"After losing my mother young, I grew up surrounded by boys. And after having two boys of my own, I was straight-up terrified of having a girl. A girl was all-new territory to me. For this mom afraid of messing up her daughter, this book is a lifeline. I might not be able to bubble wrap my girl away from the world, but I sure can wrap her up in fierce prayers and send her out into it bravely. Each prayer, each activity, each new way of seeing my girl with Jesus' eyes filled me with gratitude and a hearty *Amen* for this book!"

—Lisa-Jo Baker, author of *Never Unfriended* and *Surprised by Motherhood*, and community manager at incourage.me

"I'm a mom of girls who feels desperate at times. The reality of what's coming their way hits me and I feel frozen. *Praying for Girls* isn't just a rally cry for prayer—it's a practical and powerful weapon I can use daily. I feel equipped and cannot wait to share it with all my friends."

—Courtney DeFeo, author of *In This House, We Will Giggle* and founder of Lil Light O' Mine

"Teri Lynne Underwood understands girls—and moms. Her book *Praying for Girls* is one you'll want to keep on your bedside table for those sleepless nights when your heart is heavy and you just can't find the words. She's found them for you and will lead you on a journey that will ultimately invite your daughter and you deeper into God's grace, love, and sovereignty."

—Sissy Goff, LPC-MHSP, director of child and adolescent counseling at Daystar Counseling Ministries and author of *Raising Girls* and *Are My Kids on Track?*

"I want my girls to be world changers. I want them to be strong. I also want them to be grace-filled seekers of truth. Meanwhile, the world is doing everything it can to claim their hearts. Teri Lynne understands that praying for our girls is never a waste of time. She reminds us in her sweet Southern style that it might be the most important part of our day."

—Stacey Thacker, author of *Fresh Out of Amazing: Opening Your Heart to God's Unexpected Invitation*

"As a mom of seven daughters, this book will be put to good use. As I pore through the pages, I'm reminded of what an honor it is to prayerfully guide my daughters into womanhood. My favorite part is the Scripture-inspired prayers. I can't recommend this book enough!"

—Tricia Goyer, *USA Today* bestselling author of over sixty books, including *Praying for Your Future Husband*

"This book makes me so happy. For years I've been asked to recommend a book about praying for girls, and now I finally can! Teri

Lynne is deeply committed to the truth of God's Word, and she understands how to apply it to godly parenting. This practical and highly usable book will change a generation of future women. As a mom raising two sons who will one day need godly wives, I'm thrilled at that possibility!"

—**Brooke McGlothlin**, co-founder of the MOB Society
(for mothers of boys) and author of *Praying for Boys*

"Raising godly girls in today's culture can feel daunting. Too often mothers focus more on the challenges rather than the solution. Teri Lynne equips moms to utilize the most powerful weapon in their parenting tool belt: prayer. . . . This book should be on every mother's nightstand!"

—**Vicki Courtney**, national speaker and bestselling author
of *5 Conversations You Must Have with Your Daughter*

"Teri Lynne has crafted a treasure! This is not the kind of book you read once and put away. This is a book you take your time with and read over and over again. You let tears fall on the pages and journal through the margins until God's truth about our daughters becomes your own."

—**Wynter Pitts**, author of *She Is Yours*
and *For Girls Like You: A Devotional for Tweens*

"There's nothing I want more than to raise daughters who love Jesus, others, and themselves—in that order. This book will help moms do just that. *Praying for Girls* will take moms on a beautiful journey of trust as we commit our girls to Him."

—**Kristen Welch**, blogger at We Are THAT Family
and author of *Raising Grateful Kids in an Entitled World*

"There's no greater honor than to be Mom to our five blessings, yet it's also filled with seasons of doubt and loneliness. Teri Lynne's warm, big-sister-like encouragement reminds us it's all going to be okay, and her profound prayers point us to the One who makes it better than okay. *Praying for Girls* is a lifesaver for girl moms."

—**Jen Schmidt**, founder of The Becoming Conference
and blogger at Balancing Beauty and Bedlam

"As a mother to seven daughters, it is a blessing to have such a relevant parenting resource. *Praying for Girls* spans the topics and heart matters that every girl faces as she grows, encouraging moms to pray over their daughters and help them through their journeys."

—**September McCarthy**, author of {*Why*} *Motherhood Matters*

Praying for Girls

Praying for Girls

ASKING GOD
FOR THE THINGS THEY **NEED MOST**

Teri Lynne Underwood

BETHANY HOUSE PUBLISHERS

a division of Baker Publishing Group
Minneapolis, Minnesota

Published by Bethany House Publishers
11400 Hampshire Avenue South
Bloomington, Minnesota 55438
www.bethanyhouse.com

Bethany House Publishers is a division of
Baker Publishing Group, Grand Rapids, Michigan

Printed in the United States of America

Library of Congress Cataloging in Publication Control Number: 2017936457

ISBN 978-0-7642-1960-3

Cover design by Dan Pitts
Cover photography by Getty Images / Emely

Author represented by the literary agency of Books & Such

17 18 19 20 21 22 23   7 6 5 4 3 2 1

For Casiday Hope,
who has graciously been the test subject
as I learned to pray for her,
and who has been the bright light
of hope and healing God used
to remind me of His deepest love.

Contents

1

The Girl in the Mirror

Crooked teeth, bottle-cap glasses, and frizzy hair. That's what she saw in the mirror. It didn't matter that she'd long since had her braces removed, gotten contacts, and learned to style her thick hair. The mirror in the bathroom might have shown the girl she was now, but the mirror in her heart could only see what she'd been.

Even now, that girl occasionally looks in the mirror and sees the twelve-year-old version of herself. I know, because I'm that girl. And maybe you are too.

Oh sure, we've grown up to be wives and moms, and we are supposed to have it all together, but deep down we have moments when we're still the awkward tween wondering if we'll ever really need a bra and if a boy will ever think we're pretty.

The other day I walked past the bathroom my sixteen-year-old daughter and I share. She hadn't closed the door all the way and I could see her pushed close to the mirror, scrutinizing every detail of her face. The look in her eyes revealed what she saw—not pretty enough, not skinny enough, not smart enough, not anything enough. My heart ached for her because I know what it is to feel the weight of *not enough.*

Sometimes the hardest part of being a girl mom is understanding all the self-doubts and insecurities my daughter faces. I used to believe that would be the easiest part, it would be what connected us. But more often than not, it doesn't. Far more than I ever dreamed, I'm right there with her—stuck in my own pool of fears and insecurities.

Dress-Up and Growing Up

Like most little girls, Casiday loved playing dress-up. The Tinkerbell costume she had when she was three was nearly threadbare when I finally packed it away. A big trunk of clothes enabled her to be every sort of character from cowgirl to cheerleader. She had an arsenal of personas from weather girl to rock star.

Her desire to play with clothes and try new styles hasn't diminished over the years. (And truthfully, she might get that from her momma.) We Underwood girls love trying out the latest hair and makeup techniques and chatting about the newest fashion trends. But the truth is, my discussions with Casiday about clothes and makeup are never the real conversations. When she asks if her outfit is cute, she's really asking if I think she's pretty. When she wonders if a new eyeliner technique will make her eyes look bigger, she's really wondering if she's enough the way she is.

The tears over a shirt that doesn't look right are less about the shirt and more about herself. So often, she feels like she doesn't look "right." During those moments when she is most distraught, I have the opportunity to speak truth over her. Sometimes, she will fall into my arms and let me hug her and stroke her hair. But far more often, she withdraws. And that's become my cue to pray. Rather than trying to reason with her, I've learned to reach out to the God who loves her far more and far better than I do.

I didn't always know to do this. When she was younger, prayer was less my first response and more my last resort. But as she's gotten older and I've, hopefully, gotten wiser, I find my words to her are far less important than His words about her.

The Gift of Prayer

The girl in my mirror isn't all she imagined she'd be at age twelve or even at age thirty. Now in my mid-forties, I sometimes wonder if what I do matters, if I'm making a difference, if I'll ever do something big. The struggle to find significance and purpose doesn't end when we leave adolescence, does it?

With every season of our daughters' lives, new questions and fears arrive. We look at our girls and we know the journey is just beginning. We want to protect them from the heartaches we faced and guide them to trust the Lord with all the worries and insecurities life will bring. And so, we pray. Or at least we try to. Let's face it, there are times when prayer is overwhelming. We wonder what to say, how to say it, and if God will hear and respond to our prayers for our girls. I'm well acquainted with those feelings and uncertainties. I also know how easy it is to get distracted when I'm praying or get lost trying to find just the right words to share my heart with God. But there's good news, friends! We don't have to be perfect pray-ers, nor do our prayers have to be perfect, because the God who hears us and loves us—and our girls—is perfect and perfectly able.

E. M. Bounds wrote, "Prayer projects faith on God, and God on the world. Only God can move mountains, but faith and prayer move God."[1] This book, full of prayers based on Scripture, is an invitation to move the heart and hand of God.

Perhaps you are in the middle of a difficult time with your daughter. Remember, prayer is a battleground where we fight *for* our children. Cry out on her behalf. Beg for wisdom. Admit your hurts and fears and concerns. There will be days when you can't even form the words to make a prayer. It's okay! Those are the times when the Holy Spirit makes sense of our groanings (Romans 8:26).

We pray because He is able to accomplish more than we could ever ask or imagine (Ephesians 3:20).

Our girls are growing up in a culture radically different from the one many of us did. I recently read that this generation is the first to have no concept of life without Wi-Fi and social media.[2] As digital natives,[3] technology shapes almost every aspect of their lives and is a key factor in how they view themselves and the world. But, even with this new reality, we moms still have the privilege and responsibility of encouraging our daughters to view life through the Word of God. Praying with and for them is one of our most vital roles—and greatest gifts. The rest of this book is designed to help you know how and what to pray for your girl in five key areas of her life: Identity, Heart, Mind, Relationships, and Purpose.

Feel free to jump from chapter to chapter, based on what season you are in with your girl. Scribble in the margins and write out the verses. Use this book as a starting point for praying for your daughter. Add to the prayers and write your own. Spend time reading over the verses and share them with your girl. Talk with her about what you're learning and how you're praying. (I've added some ideas for this at the end of each chapter.) And don't be surprised if you find yourself praying some of these for yourself. After all, before you were a mom, you were a girl too.

PART 1

Prayers for Her Identity

God declares who we are in Him. He calls us chosen, beloved, precious, the apple of His eye. And yet, our girls struggle to believe these descriptors, listening instead to the words culture assigns to them. Our prayers can be the impetus our girls need to walk confidently in their identity in Christ, providing them with a solid foundation upon which they can stand when all of life is unsteady and uncertain.

In this part of the book, we'll explore four key aspects of our identity in Christ. As moms, we can help our girls walk in the truth of who they are and why they matter. By encouraging them to embrace the fullness of their identities in Christ, we equip them to stand firm and live with confidence as children of God.

Image-Bearer

May she absorb the rich truth
that she is made in the image of God.

So God created man in his own image, in the image of God he created him; male and female he created them.

Genesis 1:27

Waiting for the basketball game to begin, Casiday and some of her fellow cheerleaders were giggling as they looked at the phone they circled around. Suddenly, my girl reached back and grabbed my phone. Within seconds my phone was back on the bleacher, but I was curious. Picking it up, I opened Instagram, figuring that's where she had been. I started scanning the photos posted by the girls in front of me and noticed I had liked one I didn't remember seeing. It's not at all unusual for Casiday to like a photo using my Instagram account, so I wasn't surprised this had transpired.

I leaned forward and said, "I see I was the ninety-ninth like on this photo." Casiday's friend laughed and said, "Yeah, I'm trying to get to a hundred and needed some more likes. You don't care, do you?"

I didn't mind, of course. It was a sweet picture of some beautiful girls. But it did remind me of how easy it is for our daughters to get lost in a sea of likes and follows and lose sight of what—and Who—truly defines them.

In a world where every picture is filtered and edited, where we carefully script every word we share, where it's easy to create a persona that barely reflects the person, our girls need to know they are, above all, image-bearers of God.

Such a churchy idea, isn't it? Countless times I've looked at my girl and reminded her she is created in the image of God. But one day she asked me, "What does that even mean?" I, with my very best Bible teacher voice, replied, "Well, it means God has made you special, unique in all of creation." She said, in her very best teenager voice, "Yeah, but what does it *really* mean?"

I didn't have a great answer for her that day. I mumbled through some phrases and ideas I'd heard all my life, and she finally seemed satisfied. But I wasn't. What does it mean that we are created in the image of God? Why is it important that we grasp this truth?

As I contemplated Casiday's questions and dug into the Word, I discovered two truths about being created in the image of God.

1. We are unlike the rest of creation.

2. We are conformed to the image of God as revealed by Christ.

Unlike the Rest of Creation

When God created the sun and moon, the land and sea, the birds and fish, He said it was good. All of it was good. He spoke every animal and blade of grass into being. But when it was time to make humans, everything changed. Humanity wasn't spoken into being—we were formed by the very hands of God.

> Then the Lord God formed the man from the dust of the ground. He breathed the breath of life into the man's nostrils, and the man became a living person.
> Then the Lord God made a woman from the rib, and he brought her to the man.
>
> Genesis 2:7, 22 NLT

Humanity was different from the very start—not created the same way, not intended for the same purpose. While all of creation was beautiful and intentional, humans were also personal, created for relationship with God. Being made in the image of God sets us apart from everything else. The days we live here on earth are not the whole of our existence.

Made for more than this life, we were intended for eternal relationship with Him. When we talk with our girls about being image-bearers, we emphasize to them that what they can see today isn't all there is.

Our girls need us to remind them of the big picture of their lives, but even more, of the biggest picture of eternity. Because we are unlike the rest of creation, we have eternity set in our hearts (Ecclesiastes 3:11). And while we cannot grasp the fullness of what that means, we know it is true. Deep inside each of us, we know this life can't be all there is—the "more" our girls are longing to find and experience is only found in relationship with Him.

Conformed to His Image

"Why is it so hard?" my twenty-year-old friend asked. "Why does being like Christ have to feel impossible?"

19

Oh, sweet one, because it is impossible! Paul told the Philippians, "And I am sure of this, that he who began a good work in you will bring it to completion at the day of Jesus Christ" (Philippians 1:6).

I shared that verse with my friend and reminded her that God does the work of changing us. We can't do it ourselves. It will take our whole lives, not completed until we see Him face-to-face.

Jesus gave us the fullest revelation of God while He walked on earth. He showed us what it is to reveal the glory of God, to walk with Him, to know His heart and plans. We follow the example of Christ, seeking to be conformed to Him. And we remind our girls that this is a process and it takes time.

Day in and day out we make the decision to abide in Him, to follow Him, to become like Him. We show our girls what this looks like by our own lives—failures and successes, mountaintops and valleys. And we pray for them to know the fullness of abiding in Him so they can become like Him.

The Game Changer

Mommas, if our girls grasp this one truth—that they are made in the image of God—it'll be a game changer. Why? Because every lie the world will throw at them is rooted in the same question the serpent asked Eve: "Did God actually say . . . ?" (Genesis 3:1).

When the world says, "You're not enough," she will know Christ is sufficient, even in her weakness and inadequacy (2 Corinthians 12:9).

When the world says, "It doesn't matter what you do, as long as you're happy," she can boldly choose to be holy, as He is holy (1 Peter 1:15).

When the world says, "What you do is insignificant," she'll be certain the Lord delights in small beginnings (Zechariah 4:10).

When the world says, "Image is everything," she will rest in the knowledge she is made in His image and being conformed to His likeness (2 Corinthians 3:18).

Every day our girls are bombarded with pictures of women who have been airbrushed, styled, and surgically enhanced. And every day they look at the face in the mirror and wonder if it's enough. Our girls need us to give them biblical truth—to say to them, time and again at every age, "God really did say you are made in His image, and that image is very good." And to pray for them, time and again at every age, to absorb the truth they are "fearfully and wonderfully made" by the God of all creation (Psalm 139:14).

PRAYERS

Lord, may _____ know her identity is found in You and rest in the knowledge she is made in Your image. (Genesis 1:27)

Lord, I pray _____ will believe Your Word about her and be confident she is "fearfully and wonderfully made." When she looks in the mirror, may she see herself as You do: a wonderful work of Your hands. (Psalm 139:14)

Lord, as _____ matures in her faith, may she be more and more conformed to the image of Christ, who is the perfect image of You. (Ephesians 4:24)

Lord, when it's hard to see anything of value in herself, may _____ remember her worth is found in You, aware of the ways you are changing her into the glorious image of Christ. (2 Corinthians 3:18)

Lord, my prayer for _____ is wisdom to see You as her Creator and walk in the "new self," sure of her place in You. (Colossians 3:10)

Lord, may _____ be confident that You are mindful of her and care for her. (Psalm 8:4)

Lord, I pray _____ will remember You created her, You formed her. As that truth settles deep into her heart and mind, may she walk with You throughout her life. (Isaiah 43:1)

Lord, it's so easy to only see the flaws in ourselves. Give _____ Your vision of her, that she may see herself as a masterpiece. (Ephesians 2:10)

Lord, on the days when _____ feels worthless (because I know those days will come), cause her to remember that You are for her. (Psalm 56:9)

Lord, though we are now imperfect reflections of Your glory, I pray _____ will find hope and boldness in the promise that she will one day be a true and perfect reflection of You. (1 John 3:2)

Just for Moms

Our girls will likely face some sort of insecurity for most of their lives. Most women I know (including myself) have our own count of likes going in our head. Probably not as obvious as the Instagram likes Casiday's friend was seeking, but there nonetheless. When we look at our girls and remind them how precious they are and what a gift it is to be made in the image of God, may we also whisper those words of truth to ourselves.

> *Lord, some days we just don't know how to keep going. The whispered lies of the enemy in our minds, and the doubts, insecurities, and fears pounding in our hearts overwhelm us. Help us, especially in those weary moments, to believe we are Your wonderful works and we have the new nature given through Christ. We need You to meet us right where we are. Remind us of Your great love for us and, just like our daughters, help us remember we are made in Your image and precious to You. Orient our hearts toward truth and fill us with Your Spirit. In Jesus' name, Amen.*

Girl Talk

For little girls—Help her pick out one thing she loves about herself and then use that to show her how she is made in God's image. For example, if she really likes her eyes, you can remind her God sees us when we are happy and when we are sad, and He cares about us. Because she is made in His image, she can see when others are happy and sad and be happy with them or hurt for their sadness.

For "middle" girls—Ask your girl to show you pictures of the people she admires and tell you what appeals to her about these people. (Be careful not to judge the people she chooses—give her freedom to be honest with you!) As she mentions the traits she sees, discuss with her how God makes each of us unique. Talk about what makes her unique. At this age, being different may be hard for her. Share Psalm 139:14 and remind her she is wonderfully made and her uniqueness is good.

For older girls—Plan a mother-daughter date with your girl. Sometimes it's easy for us to get disconnected from our daughters as they get older and busier with their friends and activities. Setting aside a specific time to connect with your girl is important during this season. Share with her a time you struggled with your identity. Ask her if she's had a time when she felt uncertain about who she is and who she's supposed to be. Read Colossians 3:10 with her. Remind her that we're all learning to know Christ and become more like Him. Point out the ways you see her growing and maturing.

3

Loved

May she be confident knowing
that she is deeply loved by God.

Because you are precious in my eyes, and honored, and I love
you . . .

Isaiah 43:4

The email arrived during a particularly difficult week. With
my due date for this book's manuscript looming in front of
me, words had become elusive. Every day I sat down to write
and embraced the age-old theory of "bum in chair" until I hit
my word count. There was a restlessness in my spirit, and much
of what I'd written, though true and encouraging, felt forced
and awkward.

Checking email was a simple way of convincing myself I was
working when, in reality, I was procrastinating. Nonetheless,
that morning I opened the email with a subject line reading,

"Prayers for girls—my prayers in a quilt." My attention piqued, I had to know what was inside.

Teri Lynne,

Thank you for the amazing resources you put out and the time and effort that goes into them. I CANNOT wait for your book! Praying focus over you as you work to that deadline.

I wanted to share briefly a project that I completed for my youngest daughter (she's just two) after Prayers for Girls inspired me to create a chapter in a section of a notebook for prayers for each of my three girls. They were all based on Scripture, and themes/key words came out of those Scriptures. For my daughter Harper, there were seventeen words that encompassed more than a hundred Scriptures, which I pray through regularly. But as a quilter, I felt the Lord place on my heart to make a "prophecy quilt." I didn't even know it was a thing (and maybe it's not, really!).

Each square that I made, I prayed over as I sewed. As I sewed, I sowed. Mostly machined, but the seventeen key words I hand-stitched, and prayed through each of the Scriptures associated with those words while I did it.

Harper is: Blessed, Chosen, Fearless, Generous, Happy, Honest, Humble, Joyful, Kind, Loved, Loving, Loyal, Precious, Saved, Secure, Strong, Wise.

I'm not sure why the Lord has asked me to share this with you, and I know you are busy so I have put it off. But this project—this legacy for Harper—comes from the Prayers for Girls ministry. Attached are some pictures of the prophecy quilt, a legacy of the Lord's love for my girl, and my dedication in praying specifics over her.

God bless you, a thousand thank-yous, and much love from the other side of the world.

xx Meghan[1]

As I read Meghan's words, tears streamed down my face. She attached photos of her quilt and had no way of knowing the color scheme she'd chosen was exactly the same as the cover of this book. God's fingerprints were all over the quilt for her daughter. But they were also all over the email to me.

Meghan's email was a gentle whisper of encouragement from the Father to this oh-so-weary mom. Meghan's quilt is a gift for her daughter. But God had a gift for me as His daughter too—a reminder of His steadfast love.

The Love of God

Paul wrote these words to the Ephesians: "So that Christ may dwell in your hearts through faith—that you, being rooted and grounded in love, may have strength to comprehend with all the saints what is the breadth and length and height and depth, and to know the love of Christ that surpasses knowledge, that you may be filled with all the fullness of God" (Ephesians 3:17–19). He wanted these believers to understand the vastness of God's love for them so they could live in its fullness.

As moms, we want the same thing for our girls. When I look at these three verses I find three important truths we can teach our girls about the love of God.

God's love is unwavering. In a world that uses the word *love* casually, our girls need to know God's love for us is nothing like the affection they might feel for mint chocolate chip ice cream. God's love is certain and unwavering. Time and again in the Psalms, we read of the steadfast love of the Lord. This love

27

is rooted in His character, not in our actions. Our daughters can be sure of their place as His children. We must point them continually to the truth that when we belong to Him, we can be confident in His love for us.

God's love is unending. Just as we can stand at the edge of the beach and look out over the ocean, unable to see where it ends, God's love for us is unending. We may never fully grasp the "breadth and length and height and depth" of His sincere affection and regard for us, but we can choose to walk in faith. As we talk with our daughters about the love of God, it is vital for us to remind them of how unfathomable it truly is. David wrote, "What is man that you are mindful of him?" (Psalm 8:4). That God's love for us is beyond our ability to comprehend is a reminder of how incredible it is for Him to call us beloved.

God's love is unsurpassable. When we talk with Casiday about how much we love her, we always say, "No one on earth loves you and wants the best for you more than we do as your parents." One of our goals has always been to make sure she knows that, as much as we love her, God loves her even more. As much as we want good things for her, God wants them more. His love for us is greater than any other love we'll ever experience. When we teach our girls to walk in this truth, we give them a solid foundation for the situations and circumstances they will face in their lives.

Wrapped Up in Love and Quilts

One night, about a week after I received the email from Meghan, I found Casiday sound asleep on the couch. She was wrapped up in a quilt Scott's grandmother had made for her using some of her T-shirts. I thought again about Meghan's quilt and all the prayers she had prayed as she sewed. I know Mamaw prayed for Casiday as she put her quilt together too. Both quilts reveal a desire to express a deep love. Both are meant as a reminder of that love.

When we pray for our girls, we are, in many ways, wrapping them up in the love of God. It's a beautiful desire to express the deep love the Father has for our girls, and it's a reminder to us that He has the same steadfast love for us as well.

PRAYERS

Lord, may _____ walk in the confidence that she is known and loved by You, precious in Your sight. (Isaiah 43:4)

Lord, it is Your love, a love that never changes and never fails, that gives us life. May _____ trust in that love and abide in You always. (Psalm 119:88)

Lord, in this world where love can fail and fall away, I pray _____ will grasp the beauty of Your everlasting love and faithfulness to her. (Jeremiah 31:3)

Lord, may the love You give to _____ be the very thing that controls her, freeing her to find her true identity and confidence in You. (2 Corinthians 5:14)

Lord, may the knowledge that Your love is steadfast be a source of strength to _____, helping her to trust in Your mercies that never end. (Lamentations 3:22)

Lord, of all the treasures we find in Your love, the greatest is this: You loved us while we were still sinners and gave

Your life for ours. I pray _____ will let this truth settle deep into her heart. (Romans 5:8)

Lord, throughout her life, _____ will find that many people allow situations and circumstances and feelings to change the love they have for her. Help her know that nothing can change or separate her from Your love. (Romans 8:38–39)

Lord, thank You for Your lavish love! I pray_____ will find comfort and certainty in the promise that she is Your child. (1 John 3:1)

Lord, as _____ faces the mountains in her life, may she look at them not as obstacles to overcome but rather as a reminder of Your love for her. (Psalm 103:11)

Lord, it will be easy for my girl to get lost in all the world offers. I pray _____ will have faith and fortitude to trust You to keep her secure in Your steadfast love. (Jude 1:21)

Just for Moms

Sometimes it's hard for us to talk to our girls about the love of God because we struggle to believe it for ourselves. (Or maybe that's just me?) Daily we battle the feelings of inadequacy, the weight of unmet expectations, and the fear of messing it all up with these daughters we love so much. It can be easy to forget the deep love God has for us. Maybe you need someone to remind you of this: You are dearly loved by the God of all creation. He made you and you are precious to Him.

Lord, every day it seems like there's a new challenge in parenting. It's easy for us to get lost in all the ways we don't measure up to the standards and expectations we have set for ourselves as moms. I do it all the time. Today, God, will You meet us right where we are and remind us that Your burden is easy and Your yoke is light? Will You help us remember that we are dearly loved by the God of all creation, treasured and held tight in Your never-ending, never-failing love? Give us confidence to release all those unreasonable expectations and impossible-to-meet standards we have for ourselves. As we loosen our grip on those things, may we find You have steadfastly held us in the grip of Your own love and tender care. In Jesus' name, Amen.

Girl Talk

For little girls—Help your girl draw a heart on a piece of paper. Tell her the heart represents her. Then draw another heart around the first one. Explain to her that you love her and want the very best for her always. Finally, draw a big heart around the first two. Share with her that the big heart represents how much God loves her, even more than you do. Talk with her about God's love and how, no matter what happens in her life, God will always love her.

For "middle" girls—Write your daughter's name, putting each letter on a new line. For each letter in her name, share something you love about her and ask her to share something she loves about herself. Once you are finished, read Isaiah 43:1–4 with her. Talk with her about how God's love for us isn't based on anything we do. He loves us because we are His.

For big girls—Invite your daughter to go for coffee or a milk-shake with you. While you are together, read Isaiah 43:1–4. Talk with your girl about what it means that God says we are precious to Him, that He loves us. Look specifically at verses two and three and talk with her about times when she's felt overwhelmed and alone. Remind her that God says He loves us and will always be with us.

Known

May she be certain she is known by God.

O Lord, you have searched me and known me!

Psalm 139:1

How does she know me?" queried Casiday. At ten, she was more cognizant of people she knew, and she recognized that the person who had spoken to her was definitely not on that list.

"She is a friend of your daddy's from high school. I'm sure she's read his posts about you on Facebook," I replied.

After pondering what I'd said for a few minutes, she looked up at me with her big eyes and emphatically stated, "That's weird!"

Until Casiday's declaration, I hadn't considered her thoughts about being known (or at least known about) by people she had never met. In that moment, I realized how much the Internet and social media were changing our idea about what it means to be known.

Growing up as the preacher's daughter, granddaughter, and even great-granddaughter, I too encountered people who felt as though they knew me because of their acquaintance with family members and stories they'd heard from the pulpit. The amount of their knowledge, though, was directly related to the depth of the relationship they had with my family members. Closer friends had access to more personal stories, while church members only knew about me in broader terms. Social media, though, changed all that.

People Scott and I haven't seen in years may have seen a photo or read a status about Casiday's latest antics. If we bump into rarely seen high school or college friends, they immediately recognize Casiday and treat her with the same familiarity as people in our everyday lives.

Known or Known About

I am a bit of a celebrity stalker. Not in a creepy way (at least I don't think it is), but in that "we'd totally be BFFs if she weren't a movie star" kind of way. Basically, I'm convinced that if I met Reese Witherspoon or Jennifer Garner at Target, we'd immediately connect. But since that scenario is extremely unlikely, I feed my fantasy by following them on social media and buying the occasional issue of *People* magazine. Reese Witherspoon is especially relatable in her social media.

But here's the thing: As much as I know about Reese, I don't know her. (And she'd probably be a little bit freaked out if we happened to bump into each other on the street in my sleepy Southern town and I started chatting with her about her favorite coffee drink or how cute the dress was that she wore while at her son's birthday party.)

Just like my daughter finds it weird that people who don't know her talk to her as if they do, I'd imagine Reese would feel similarly about me assuming a familiarity based on a few pictures and articles I've seen.

When we only know *about* someone, we can easily be disenchanted by his or her poor choices or inappropriate actions. Consider how the media is quick to vilify the very stars it creates. Knowing about another person isn't a relationship. But when we take time to get to know someone, we are building a relationship. I am not friends with Reese Witherspoon, no matter how much I know about her.

Living Known

God doesn't just know *about* us. He knows us. In fact, He knows us better than we know ourselves and far better than anyone else does. In Psalm 139:1 David says, "O Lord, you have searched me and known me!"

Truly being known by others is rare. We long for someone to "get" us. I believe this is a God-given desire intended to draw us closer to Him. When David speaks of God knowing him, it's not just an existential idea. David recognizes God is intimately aware of every detail of his life.

> You know when I sit down and when I rise up;
> you discern my thoughts from afar.
> You search out my path and my lying down
> and are acquainted with all my ways.
> Even before a word is on my tongue,
> behold, O Lord, you know it altogether.
> Psalm 139:2–4

Just as God knew the details of David's comings and goings, thoughts and desires, He knows our daughters. And His knowledge is complete, perfect. He knows their failures and their successes. He sees the desires of their hearts—good and bad. He knows every struggle and every victory. And what He knows doesn't change His plan and love for them.

What a gift it is for us, as moms, to remind them of this good Father who knows them not from Facebook status updates but because He is the One who made them!

PRAYERS

Lord, thank You for the hope we have in being known by You! I pray _____ will find refuge in the assurance that You have searched and known her. (Psalm 139:1)

Lord, may _____ find comfort in the truth that You know what we need before we even ask. May she come to You in prayer with certainty that she is welcomed into Your presence. (Matthew 6:8)

Lord, when life is hard and she feels unknown, unseen, and unloved, please help _____ remember You are the God who knows her, who sees her, and who loves her. (Genesis 16:13)

Lord, with all my heart I pray my girl loves You and knows Your love. And as _____'s relationship with You grows, may she love You more and rest in the peace that You know her. (1 Corinthians 8:3)

Lord, thank you for the truth that you are interested in every detail of our lives. May _____ rest in the assurance that You see her comings and goings and you are "acquainted with all her ways." (Psalm 139:3)

Lord, when the ground is shaky beneath her feet, I pray
_____ will trust in You as her firm foundation,
sure she is sealed by You. (2 Timothy 2:19)

Lord, when _____ faces the days of trouble, may
she turn to You, trusting in Your strength and refuge.
(Nahum 1:7)

Lord, just as You knew Jeremiah before he was formed in his
mother's womb, You also knew my girl. I pray _____
will, like Jeremiah, be faithful to the path and plan You
have for her life. (Jeremiah 1:5)

Lord, there will be nights when she can't stop the tears
from flowing. In those dark hours, I pray _____
will remember that You keep every tear, know every toss
and turn, and hold her close. (Psalm 56:8)

Lord, You are the Good Shepherd, the gentle Guide for
those who love You. I pray _____ will always hear
Your voice and be certain You know her. (John 10:14)

Just for Moms

Casiday's mom. Scott's wife. Terry and Sue's daughter. Sandra's friend.

Ever feel like you are only known by your relationship to
others? I guess it's just a part of life, and especially of motherhood. I can remember being called "Mrs. Casiday's mom" by
more than one child at the preschool my girl attended.

I'm thankful for all the relationships that have become a part
of who I am, but sometimes I just want to be me, Teri Lynne.
No one's wife, no one's mom. Just plain ol' me. You too? Good

news, my friend. When it comes to the Lord, we are truly and fully known.

Lord, sometimes we moms feel a little bit unnoticed, unless someone needs something. It seems as though our names are only used in connection with requests for reading a book or getting a snack or finding a missing uniform piece. Sometimes, if we were really honest, we'd say we think we are known only for what we can do for others. Help us remember that in You we are fully known. Every detail of our days, every hair on our heads, every worry on our hearts, every tear in our eyes, everything about us and inside us is known by You. You know who we are and who we long to be. When we lose sight of this truth, will You gently draw us back to You? Help us walk in the freedom of being known by the God who sees, and give us grace as we serve our families. In Jesus' name, Amen.

Girl Talk

For little girls—Using a mirror, ask your girl what she sees about herself (her hair, eye color, clothes, etc.). Share with her what you see when you look at her, including attributes of her character and personality (kindness, sense of humor, etc.) that can't be seen in the mirror. Read Psalm 139:14 and explain to her that God doesn't just see what's on the outside like she could see in the mirror or even what you see when you look at her. God sees everything about her, and He loves her.

For "middle" girls—Ask your girl who her favorite celebrity is. Now ask her questions about that person. Be sure to include questions she will know the answers to as well as things she won't know. Talk with her about the difference between knowing someone and knowing about someone. Share with her how social media can make it seem like we really know someone when the truth is, we just know the parts about them they let us see. Read Jeremiah 1:5 with her. Discuss what it means that God knew us even before we were born. Remind her how much God loves her, that He really knows her and that she is precious to Him.

For big girls—Plan another mother-daughter date with your girl. Sometimes getting away from the normal routine at home is the best way to open the door to deeper conversation. But remember to give her space to consider what you are discussing and accept that she may not have a quick answer. The point is to help her learn to think about her life in light of God's Word. Ask your girl how many people she thinks really know her. Be honest about any struggles you have with being known or feeling unnoticed. Talk with her about the difference between knowing someone and knowing about someone. Read Psalm 139:1–6 with her and remind her that she isn't just some random person to God. He knows her, and He loves her.

Accepted

May she rest in the full acceptance of God.

You did not choose me, but I chose you and appointed you that you should go and bear fruit and that your fruit should abide, so that whatever you ask the Father in my name, he may give it to you.

John 15:16

You know, when we first met, I didn't like you at all."

Valerie has the whole story of our first meeting perfectly timed to give maximum comedic impact. Her impersonation of my "Hi! I'm Teri Lynne Underwood!" over the pew at Blythe Island Baptist Church is hilarious (though I still contend I was not nearly as peppy or obnoxious as she claims).

We laugh about it now because after twelve years of friendship, it seems crazy to think that at first glance Val was 100 percent certain we could never be friends. But friends we are. In fact, Valerie has walked with me, prayed with me, and held me up during some of the most difficult seasons of my life. She has seen me at my very worst and stayed by my side. I'm thankful her first impression didn't keep us from the friendship we now share.

Val and I can joke now, but the truth is, there is a deep relief inside me that she didn't just write off the worship leader's obnoxious wife that Sunday so many years ago. I could tell other stories with much different endings.

The Sting of Rejection

My first recollection of not being chosen was in sixth grade. I tried out for the basketball team. Rather than rehash the whole traumatic tale, let's just say dribbling while running wasn't my thing. Honestly, I didn't really want to play basketball. But it was my first year at a new school and I thought it would help me find a place to belong, an opportunity to be accepted.

Instead, I was the clumsy new girl.

In the thirty-plus years since, the sting of rejection has come around more often than I'd like. And I bet you have known it too.

This is where it gets hard. Because we know how much it hurts to not be accepted, not be chosen, we want our girls never to experience that heartache.

But we know they will.

How do we prepare our girls to deal with the inevitable rejection they will face? How do we help them settle in their hearts and minds the truth that they are chosen by God? (Especially when we aren't always confident of it ourselves.)

Two of the best tools we have for guiding and teaching our daughters are story and Scripture. When we can share our own stories with them, we remind them they are not alone and that we understand more than they think we do. (Trust me, if you have a little girl, there will come a day when you'll want her to know you aren't completely out of touch with the world she lives in.)

But our stories are most powerful when we use them to point to biblical truth. One of the best examples of how Jesus meets us in our rejection is the woman at the well. In John 4, we meet a Samaritan woman, filling her water jars in the heat of the day. She's getting her water in the middle of the day which, according to the customs of the time, reveals she is, at the very least, uncomfortable around the other women in her village.

Grab your Bible and read John 4:1–45 to refresh your memory of this encounter. I'll wait here.

When Others Reject, Jesus Accepts

So good, right? I love what we see about how Jesus responds when we feel rejected.

First, He chooses to meet us where we are. Note in verse 4 where it says, "He *had* to pass through Samaria" (emphasis added). Geographically, Jesus could have traveled from Judea to Galilee without going through Samaria. But He didn't. Jesus' compassion compelled Him to be where the need was.

Second, He chooses to see us as we are. In the familiar conversation, we learn that Jesus knows the woman has been married five times and now lives with a sixth man who isn't her husband (verses 17–18). Can you imagine the look on her face? But I believe that since she stayed with Him to talk, she recognized something different about this itinerant teacher. There is something deeply comforting about being seen as we are and accepted anyway.

Third, He chooses us based on His character, not ours. Jesus didn't spend a lot of time rehashing all the woman's sins, nor did He point out what she could do to make the situation better. Instead, He helped her focus on who He is and what He offered her.

Fourth, when we believe He chooses us, we are changed. Jesus offered her Living Water and she was changed! After her encounter with Jesus, she went and told the very people she'd been working so hard to avoid, "Come, see a man who told me all that I ever did!" (verse 29). And they did! And they too were changed (verse 39).

Our daughters long to be accepted, to be chosen. Little girls want to know how much you love them. Big girls want to be reassured they can't do anything to lose your love. And friend, deep inside, you know that need too. We all do.

It's funny now to think about Valerie's first impression of me. I joke that I must be an acquired taste. But isn't it sweet to know that Jesus' acceptance of us isn't rooted in who we are but in who He is? A sweet promise both our girls and we need to believe and cherish.

PRAYERS

Lord, I pray _____ knows she has been chosen by You and purposed to share the light You have placed inside her as she tells of Your great love. (1 Peter 2:9)

Lord, may _____ walk in the knowledge she is dearly loved by You and, out of that acceptance, may she also be compassionate, kind, and willing to accept others. (Colossians 3:12)

Lord, we live in an ungodly, decidedly unholy world. Grant _____ the boldness and confidence to live as one who has been chosen, pursuing holiness in her life as she follows You. (Ephesians 1:4)

Lord, I pray _____ will walk in the freedom of being chosen and accepted by You. May that freedom lead her to love and serve others, following Your example. (Galatians 5:13)

Lord, thank You for choosing me! I pray _____ will know that You have also chosen her, and out of that knowledge she will be faithful to bear fruit for You. (John 15:16)

Lord, when she wanders from the path You have for her, I pray _____ will know You watch for her return, full of compassion and kindness, and she is always welcomed by You. (Luke 15:20)

Lord, You have engraved _____'s name on Your palms. May she know that Your love and acceptance are permanent and based on Your promise, not her performance. (Isaiah 49:16)

Lord, when she feels unaccepted by the people around her, I pray _____ will call on You and realize You are near to her. (Psalm 145:18)

Lord, I pray _____ will know You are always with her. In the hard seasons, when shadows fall upon her path, may she remember You have chosen her and You will never leave her. (Psalm 23:4)

Lord, Your Word says that when we draw near to You, You will draw near to us. May _____ make it the habit of her life to walk in that promise, drawing ever nearer to You. (James 4:8)

Just for Moms

I shared about how Valerie didn't think she and I could be friends, but we are. But I have another story without that sort of ending. One time a church member told me she hated me and it had kept her from coming to church. As a pastor's wife, can I just tell you that is my worst nightmare! The idea that something I say or do could cause people to leave our church is horrifying. And while the woman and I did work through the situation, it wasn't easy.

It has taken me several years to move past that experience. All the insecurities and fears I have about being liked and accepted came to the forefront. I clung to verses like 1 Peter 2:9, a reminder that I am chosen by God. But the one I loved the most was Psalm 23:4, the simple reminder and profound truth, "You are with me." No matter what happens around me, no matter who likes me or doesn't, no matter what the world says, God is with me. He has chosen me. And He has chosen you too.

Lord, You know the sting of rejection. You know what it is to be betrayed by those You love. When our hearts ache and we are weighed down by feeling unaccepted and unchosen, You ache with us. We all have our own heartbreaks and struggles. We can never know the fullness of another mom's fears and aches. But You do. And You have given all of us the same promise I have clung to in my own seasons of rejection—You are with us. You have chosen us, called us by name. We are Yours. May we rest in this truth and find comfort in Your presence. In Jesus' name, Amen.

Girl Talk

For little girls—Read "See, I have written your name on the palms of my hands. . . ." (Isaiah 49:16 NLT) with your daughter. Explain to her that God has written our names on His hand as a sign of His unending love and care for us. Ask her how it makes her feel that God has her name on His hand. Using a marker, draw a heart on her palm and on yours as a reminder that God loves and chooses us.

For "middle" girls—Ask your girl if she has ever felt left out. Share with her about a time when you felt rejected. It's important that girls at this age hear us talk about hard things, but also that we consistently point them back to Christ and to the Word. Remind her that God chooses us and accepts us. Using James 4:8, remind her that when she feels rejected, the best response is to draw near to God and to pray.

For big girls—This conversation with your girl may not be easy. Prepare yourself that she may not be willing to share her own experiences with you, and choose not to take that personally. As our daughters get older, rejection will be a real part of their experience, and it is important for us as moms to give them space to process their feelings and responses. Plan to do something with your girl, maybe baking cookies or going for a walk. Ask her if she's ever felt left out or rejected by her friends. Talk with her about your own experiences of rejection and how they have hurt you. Remind your daughter that Jesus was also rejected by His friends and knows how that feels. If she isn't open to talking much, it's okay! Write out Ephesians 1:4 for her and leave it as a note on her bed.

PART 2

Prayers for Her Heart

I t's no secret our girls are often guided by their feelings. The world tells them to follow their hearts, but we know the dangers that can bring. The Bible speaks clearly about our hearts and what God desires for them. As we pray for our daughters' hearts, we long for them to be guided by the eternal Word rather than ever-changing feelings.

In these chapters, we'll explore what the Bible says about our hearts and how we can pray for our girls not to be ruled by their feelings but rather to filter their emotions through the truth of Scripture. Our prayers are a powerful instrument for shaping our girls' hearts to mirror the heart of Christ.

Pure

May she desire and pursue a pure heart.

Blessed are the pure in heart, for they shall see God.

Matthew 5:8

Katy is one of those people who shines Jesus. I'm sure you know what I mean. She is beautiful and gracious, but even more, her countenance glows. Joy exudes from her smile, and kindness flows in her words. There is a naiveté about her, an innocence. More than once I've heard her described as the kind of girl you hope your daughter grows up to become and the kind you hope your son marries.

Over the years I've known Katy, she's faced some hard seasons. She's stood for Jesus when no one around her was doing so. She's given her heart to people who haven't treasured it. She's known the hurt of loneliness and betrayal. And yet, there is still something about her. Something we don't see much in this world—a pure heart.

A Mary Heart

I think very few people really saw Jesus. Oh, they saw what He did. They saw the healing and the baskets of food and the turned-over temple tables. But, for the most part, they missed seeing Jesus, this God-made-Man who walked among them.

When I read the Gospels, I always find myself intrigued by Jesus' location. I like to know where He was when specific events happened, where He performed miracles, and what places He visited most often. It doesn't take much observation to recognize Bethany, located just a few miles outside Jerusalem, as a place He liked to be. Jesus was often in this city, and while there, He liked to stay with His friends: Mary, Martha, and Lazarus.

We know He felt a strong attachment to all three of these siblings. But there was something about Mary. I think, in many ways, Mary understood what Jesus was saying more than most. Her contemplative nature gave her insight and wisdom others may have missed. When I look at the words He spoke to and about her, it's clear Jesus saw the purity of her heart.

We first meet Mary in Luke 10, when Jesus and His disciples visit the home she shares with her siblings, Martha and Lazarus. While Martha was busy preparing a meal for the traveling men, Mary was sitting at Jesus' feet listening to Him teach. Martha, tired of doing all the work herself, barged up to Jesus and told Him (TOLD Him! Can you even imagine?) to make Mary come help her. Jesus, with equal parts toughness and tenderness, spoke to the huffy Martha about her sister, "Martha, Martha, you are anxious and troubled about many things, but one thing is necessary. Mary has chosen the good portion, which will not be taken away from her" (Luke 10:41–42).

We could spend a lot of time on Martha and what Jesus was saying to her. But for now, let's look at what He said about

Mary. First, she chose what mattered in the moment. Martha was worried about all the people and meeting their needs. Mary saw the Person of Christ and knew her own need. Second, she chose what mattered for eternity. Jesus said Mary's portion would be hers forever.

In John 11 we meet Mary and Martha again. Their brother, Lazarus, had died and been buried. The sisters sent word to Jesus before Lazarus died, but He didn't come until after the burial. Heartbroken, both sisters spoke the same words to Jesus, "If you had been here, my brother would not have died" (John 11:21, 32). Jesus reminded Martha that He is the resurrection and life and all who believe in Him will live again. But to Mary, His response was far different.

When Jesus saw her weeping, and the Jews who had come with her also weeping, He was deeply moved in His spirit and greatly troubled (John 11:32).

He already knew He would raise Lazarus for the glory of God. He told His disciples before they went to Bethany what would happen (John 11:14–15). Mary's tears, her grief and sorrow, didn't move Jesus to speak; they moved Him to weep (verse 35). Once again, we see Jesus touched by the authenticity of Mary's heart.

The final encounter between Jesus and Mary is where we grasp the fullness of what it is to live with a pure heart. Take a moment to read Matthew 26:6–13 and John 12:1–7.

Characteristics of a Pure Heart

In this third exchange between Jesus and Mary, we find three vital truths about a pure heart. As we pray for our daughters and as we teach them to have a passion for Christ, these are three characteristics we need to pursue for ourselves and to encourage in our girls.

A pure heart is extravagant. The oil with which Mary anointed Jesus was expensive. Matthew and John both note the material worth of the ointment, about a year's wages. This reminds me of the widow's mite in Luke 21. Jesus said she gave all that she had to live on (Luke 21:4). Mary held nothing back from Jesus. Her gift was costly because her love was great.

A pure heart is evident. When Mary opened that bottle and then poured its contents on Jesus' head and feet, the smell filled the room. John says, "The house was filled with the fragrance of the perfume" (John 12:3). When we are devoted to the Lord, when our hearts are pure before Him, it's evident. The sacrifices in the Old Testament were a fragrant aroma to the Lord, and so too are we. Paul wrote, "For we are the aroma of Christ to God among those who are being saved and among those who are perishing" (2 Corinthians 2:15). Just as the smell of Mary's perfume filled the house, a pure heart is the aroma of Christ to those around us.

A pure heart is earnest. In Matthew's gospel, Jesus described Mary's act of worship in this way: "She has done a beautiful thing to me" (26:10). Her actions were motivated solely by love and adoration. Mary wasn't seeking attention for herself, only to worship her Savior. Jesus recognized her purity of heart by saying, "Truly, I say to you, wherever this gospel is proclaimed in the whole world, what she has done will also be told in memory of her" (v. 13). A pure heart is focused on giving glory to God, not drawing glory to self.

When I think about Katy, it isn't her outward beauty that comes to mind (though she is a lovely young woman). Rather, my thoughts fill with her manner of living, humbly and honestly, always seeking to point to the Lord. I'm thankful for the influence she has in my daughter's life, and I pray Casiday will be an example to others in the same way.

PRAYERS

Lord, the world will push _____ toward all manner of unsatisfying and unholy things. When the allure of those things is strong, I pray she will remember You have given her a new heart, a heart of flesh, guided by Your Spirit at work inside her. (Ezekiel 36:26)

Lord, You have said that those who are pure in heart are blessed because they are the ones who can truly see You. May _____ understand and pursue purity of heart in order that she may clearly follow You for her whole life. (Matthew 5:8)

Lord, I pray _____ will be committed to Your Word. May she live in the protection of Your statutes and know that Your way is meant to guide and protect her heart and life. (Psalm 119:9)

Lord, as _____ matures, she will face the constant tension between seeking You and following the world. I pray she will make the choice to flee the sinful things culture puts in front of her and determine to choose righteousness in every aspect of her life. (2 Timothy 2:22)

Lord, I know how important it is to have godly friends. I pray _____ will be wise about those she allows into her confidence and will seek those friendships rooted in obedience to You. (1 Peter 1:22)

Lord, it's easy to begin to think that what makes sense to us is right. May you give _____ wisdom to seek You and allow You to guide her path. (Proverbs 16:2)

Lord, I pray _____ will learn early the simple truth that You are less concerned about what she does and more interested in the state of her heart. May she desire to remain pure before You and recognize the value of a broken and contrite heart in confession. (Psalm 51:17)

Lord, when _____ sins, when she veers from the path You have laid out for her, will You remind her of Your faithful love and Your readiness to forgive. May she quickly return to You, trusting in the promise of Your grace and mercy. (Joel 2:12)

Lord, just like the woman who anointed Jesus with the contents of her alabaster flask, may _____ have a heart that seeks to do beautiful things for You. I pray she will live sacrificially and humbly for Your glory. (Matthew 26:10)

Lord, may _____ dwell in Your love. May her heart be ruled by the peace You offer, and may she give freely of Your love to those around her. (Colossians 3:15)

Just for Moms

"But Jesus, aware of this, said to them, 'Why do you trouble the woman? For she has done a beautiful thing to me'" (Matthew 26:10).

I love this verse. It has nestled deep inside me over the past year. One of my desires is to be a woman who does beautiful things for the Lord. But if I'm honest, some days my desire gets overshadowed by the dishes and the demands. Life gets crowded, doesn't it?

One of the ways I keep my heart pure and focused on the Lord is by memorizing Scripture. When I'm washing dishes or running errands, I recite the verses I've learned. Keeping the Word rolling around my head helps my heart. I can't explain why or even how, but I know it does. May I invite you to try the same thing? Maybe start with Matthew 26:10, and as you memorize it, ask God to help your life be devoted to doing beautiful things to Him.

Lord, we want pure hearts and to offer You the fragrant aroma of lives lived for You. We desire to do beautiful things to You. But, honestly, in between the diapers and dishes, the dusting and driving, our best intentions get lost in the shuffle. So here we are, asking You to help us. Today, we are asking for an extra measure of grace. Will You meet us in the middle of all the mess and show us Your glory? You are generous and gracious, we know that. You promise to give us the desires of our hearts. The desire for a pure heart, a heart like Yours, is Your plan for us. Lord, give us a special dose of Your presence today. And help us do a beautiful thing to You. In Jesus' name, Amen.

Girl Talk

For little girls—Let your daughter choose a bottle of body spray and a stuffed animal to purchase at the dollar store. Let her spray some of the body spray on herself and talk about what it smells like. Open the bottle and let her pour it all on the stuffed animal. Discuss how much stronger the smell is. Walk with her through your house as she carries the animal. Talk with her about the way the aroma fills the whole house. Tell her that when we love Jesus, our kindness and love for Him spreads all around us, just like the fragrance of the body spray spread around the animal.

For "middle" girls—Wrap up a bottle of scented lotion and give it to your girl. Tell her you want to do something special with her before she goes to bed. As she gets ready to climb into bed, use the lotion on her hands and feet. (A lavender or vanilla scent will be especially soothing.) As you massage, share why you love her and what makes her special to you. Talk with her about Mary anointing Jesus as a way of showing her love for Him. Note how the fragrance of the lotion has filled up the room you are in. Pray with her that she will be the fragrance of Christ to those around her.

For big girls—Give your daughter a manicure or pedicure. As you carefully massage her hands or feet with lotion, tell her how you see her heart shining for Jesus lately. While you paint her nails, tell her the story of Mary anointing Jesus. Be sure to share with her His words, "She has done a beautiful thing to me." While her nails are drying, discuss ways she can do beautiful things for Him. Pray with her that as she strives to look beautiful on the outside, may she never forget the beauty of a pure heart for Christ.

7

Kept

May she be faithful
to keep her heart focused on God.

Keep your heart with all vigilance, for from it flow the springs of life.

Proverbs 4:23

Please, keep track of the time," I said, as I left my girl to run some errands.

"I will, Mom."

Famous last words.

When I got home about an hour later, Casiday was still on the couch, right where she had been when I left. Her "I'm sorry" didn't change the fact that we were now going to be late to meet her daddy for dinner. While she quickly changed clothes and as we drove to the restaurant, I lectured her on responsibility and common courtesy.

Just like Casiday failed to keep track of time, there are times when our girls (and their moms) will forget to keep their hearts guarded and protected. One definition of *keep* is "to maintain (some action), especially in accordance with specific requirements, a promise, etc."[1] The admonition to keep our hearts with all vigilance is a reminder to maintain our alignment with God's Word.

How do we encourage our girls to keep their hearts with all vigilance in a world that tells them, "Life is short! Follow your heart"?

When I told Casiday to keep track of the time, I knew she had the tools she needed to do so. There are clocks all over our house, and she has one on her phone (which might be permanently attached to her hand). Not only did she have the tools, she also had the skills. She knows how to tell time, and she is aware of how to determine how much time she has to accomplish a task.

Just like my girl had the tools and skills she needed to follow my instructions, God has given us the tools and skills we need to heed His guidelines in our lives. Our most important tool is the Bible. Scripture provides us with His desire for our lives. As we study and learn Scripture, we gain the skills we need to abide in Him and obey His directions for our lives.

Psalm 119 is a great place to learn more about the Word of God and how we can use it in our lives as we seek to follow Christ. As I look at this passage, I find three important ways Scripture helps us keep our hearts with all vigilance.

Treasure the Word

Remember Katy from the last chapter? When she was in high school, she had a very long bus ride to and from school. Every morning she got on the bus around 6:30. At first, she had a hard time figuring out how to spend time in the Word when she had to leave for school so early. But by the second week of school, she realized God had given her an hour every morning while she was on the bus.

Katy knew the importance of God's Word in her life. She was committed to making her daily devotions a priority, even if that meant reading her Bible on the school bus. Katy had learned early in her life the truth of Psalm 119:103–105:

> How sweet are your words to my taste, sweeter than
>   honey to my mouth!
> Through your precepts I get understanding; therefore I
>   hate every false way.
> Your word is a lamp to my feet and a light to my path.

If we want our girls to keep their hearts with all vigilance, we need to teach them to treasure the Word of God. We can do this by setting an example for them in our own lives, and also by helping them develop the habit of daily devotions for themselves.

Trust the Word

As our girls learn to treasure Scripture, we must help them move to the next step in having a kept heart: trusting the Word. It's one thing to know God's Word; it's another to know it is true and trustworthy for ourselves. One of the best ways to help our girls learn to trust God's Word is by sharing with them the times He has proven true and faithful in our lives.

For example, a friend of mine prayed for God to prune from her daughter's life the people who might distract her from following Him. Over time, her daughter's friends one by one fell away. It was a hard season for both mother and daughter, but in the end, God brought new friendships that honored Him into the girl's life. Her mom shared from her own prayer journal how she had prayed for the pruning and the new friends and what Scriptures she had prayed. This helped her daughter understand the way God works and how His Word is proven true time and again.

Psalm 119:7 says, "I will praise you with an upright heart, when I learn your righteous rules." As our girls learn to trust in the Word, they will also grow in their understanding of the faithfulness of God. What better way to teach them to keep their hearts in Him than to encourage them to see His faithfulness in their lives.

Talk the Word

Do you ever have to repeat something multiple times in order for your girl to respond? I'm sure I'm not the only one who has a child with selective hearing. It's frustrating, isn't it, repeating our instructions?

How many times a day do you tell your girl you love her or how special she is to you? We don't mind repeating that, do we? We want them to hear over and over how much they mean to us, how precious they are. The psalmist had the same desire to continually speak of the Lord.

Seven times a day I praise you for your righteous rules.

Psalm 119:164

When our girls hear us speaking the Word and applying it to the situations we face in life, they learn how they can do the same. When we encourage them with Scripture and invite them to study and memorize with us, we show them the value of praising the Lord throughout our days.

PRAYERS

Lord, sometimes it's hard to know what's going on in my girl's heart but I know that You see it all. I pray _____ _____ will be wise to guard her heart, to keep it safe with all vigilance. May she realize how important it is to protect her heart and keep it devoted to You. (Proverbs 4:23)

Lord, may _____'s heart be focused on building Your kingdom, not her own. May she learn early the value of pursing righteousness, and trust in the blessings and provision she receives as she abides in You. (Matthew 6:33)

Lord, the hard days will come for _____. I pray that during those times, she will remember she is not alone, that You are always with her and that You have overcome. May she know the peace and comfort of Your presence at all times, in all seasons. (John 16:33)

Lord, when the world lets her down and her friends don't show up, I pray _____ will remember You are faithful. May she trust in You always, certain of Your love for her. (Psalm 31:14)

Lord, may _____ remember to cast all the worries and fears and cares and struggles she faces on You. I pray she is confident in the knowledge that You care deeply for her. May she never doubt that You are willing and able to carry the burdens in her life. (1 Peter 5:7)

Lord, I pray _____'s eyes are kept on You. May she look to You and wait on You. When life feels hard, keep her heart focused on You. May she be confident You hear her and love her. (Micah 7:7)

Lord, I know there will be days when _____ deals with insecurity and uncertainty, days when she questions her own value. When those days come, Lord, will You remind her that she can come to You with all boldness and confidence? Remind her of the grace and mercy You offer in her times of need. (Hebrews 4:16)

Lord, the enemy wants _____ to be afraid. He's going to do all he can to keep her faith small and her fears large. But I pray boldly that she will walk in Your Spirit, certain of the power, love, and self-control You give her in all things. (2 Timothy 1:7)

Lord, it's easy to stay busy in our frantic world. And as _____ gets older, there will be more and more distractions in her life. I pray she will know the value of being still before You and find that, as she does, she knows the fullness of who You are. (Psalm 46:10)

Lord, _____ will have to deal with people who don't like her. Some may have reason and some may not. But the reality is, they will be a part of her life. I pray she will remember when these situations come that You are always near, always for her. (Psalm 56:9)

Just for Moms

Right now I have several friends in the middle of very difficult seasons. Some are fighting for their marriages, some for their health, and others are desperate for their prodigal children to return to the Lord. There are no easy words of encouragement and no simple answers to the complexities of life. But I've found that when I center my prayers in the Word, I am better able to guard my heart from all the human emotions that keep me from walking in faith.

Maybe you are in the middle of a battle that seems overwhelming. Perhaps you too struggle to guard your heart from all the confusion and doubt the enemy likes to send our way. You're not alone. We've all been there, are there, or will likely be there again.

Lord, some days it's hard to keep our focus on You. We want to treasure Your Word, to store it up in our hearts as protection against sin and doubt and worry and fear. But, the thing is, we get busy and distracted. And sometimes, the weight of the world feels like too much for us to bear. You know that feeling far better than we ever will. Help us remember that truth. No matter what situations we face in this life, You are with us. You invite us to cast our cares on You, secure in the knowledge that You care for us. Draw us close to You and give us wisdom to keep our hearts with all vigilance, to trust in Your Word and Your character even in the hardest moments of our days. I pray You will bring others to speak truth and hope into our lives and give us the opportunity to do the same for those in our circles of influence. In Jesus' name, Amen.

Girl Talk

For little girls—Create a treasure box with your daughter. Help her find items she can keep in her box and talk with her about what she treasures. Tell her that we all have a treasure box in our hearts. We fill them up with memories and words and even pictures of the people and moments that are special to us. Remind her that God's Word is a treasure to us and that it's important that we keep it in our hearts.

For "middle" girls—Take some time to show your girl what's in your jewelry box. Share with her why the different pieces you have are special to you. Talk about any of the pieces you especially value. Share Proverbs 4:23 with her. Remind her that her heart is a treasure box, and that she needs to be careful about what fills it.

For big girls—Take your daughter out for a coffee date (or smoothie or milkshake, whatever she loves). Share Psalm 119:104 with her. Talk with her about how you invest time in Bible study and how knowing God's Word has helped you learn to guard your heart and keep it in line with God's will. Ask her how you can help her continue to grow and have a better understanding of the Bible. Pray with her that she will keep her heart close to the Lord.

8

Content

May she be content in God
and in the plans He has for her.

For where your treasure is, there your heart will be also.

Matthew 6:21

But I neeeed it!" she said, stamping her chubby little legs in front of the latest Shopkins set. I stood there, trying not to laugh, as my friend leaned down to explain to her daughter the difference between *want* and *need*.

"You don't *need* it, sweetie, you *want* it. And today, we're not buying Shopkins. Remember when we discussed this in the car?"

Sarah looked up at her mom and slowly said, "You had the discussion. I just sat there."

Again, trying to restrain the giggle inside, I looked at my friend and shrugged my shoulders. I'd been in the car with them, and the girl had a point—Sarah was sitting quietly while her mom explained the purpose of the trip to Target, but she never expressed her own agreement. But her mom's point was far more significant—and much harder to grasp.

My friend wanted her daughter to understand two things: contentment with what she already had, and life isn't always about her. None of us really enjoy learning those lessons, do we?

Contentment Doesn't Come Naturally

Let's face it, there's a little discontent in all of us. If you have straight hair you wish it were curly. If you're short you wish you were tall. The list can go on forever. Being content doesn't come naturally for us.

Consider Adam and Eve. They had it all. Their life really was perfect. They had a beautiful garden, meaningful work, and an intimate relationship with God. Yet all it took was the implication by the serpent that they were missing out on something, and suddenly everything they had paled in comparison with what they didn't.

They believed the enemy's lie that God didn't have their best interests in mind, that He was somehow holding out on them. They bit the fruit. And we've been biting it ever since. Little girls want Shopkins, teenage girls want to be popular, and moms want to be like Susie Homemaker who posts daily images of her family's prayer time on Instagram.

When Sarah looked at those shelves in Target, she could easily point out all she already had. But her five-year-old eyes were focused on what she didn't have. And it consumed her. As my friend explained to her little girl that she didn't need any new Shopkins (and she wasn't getting one), she was laying the foundation for one of the most important lessons we learn as believers: to be content.

Learning Contentment

Scott and I had been married for about two years when we decided we were ready to have a baby. (Yes, I too chuckle at the idea of being "ready" for kids. If we'd only known, right?) Like most people, we just assumed once we had made that decision, we'd be happily expecting within a few months. Instead, we spent two more years taking tests and temperatures, counting days, and having doctor visits. On a Wednesday in March 1999, a specialist in Birmingham, Alabama, spoke the most heartbreaking words we could hear: "I just don't believe you'll ever have a baby of your own."

We drove the two hours back home to north Alabama and went to church that night, barely holding back our tears. We had choir practice, and one of the songs we rehearsed was "God Is the Strength of My Heart," a praise song based on Psalm 73:26: "My flesh and my heart may fail, but God is the strength of my heart and my portion forever."

As we sang, the emptiness in our hearts felt magnified. Over the following weeks, the ache was, at times, unbearable. Our flesh and hearts were failing. Individually and as a couple we grappled with several big questions. If this is God's plan for our lives, do we still believe He is good? Is God the strength of our hearts? Is there nothing we desire besides Him?

We wrestled through our doubts and fears. We prayed and we cried. We held on to each other and to our faith. Ultimately, we reached the point of saying, "No matter what, God is good. We trust His plan for us, and we choose to believe He will give us the strength we need."

At the time, I didn't realize we were learning to be content, but we surely were. We, in our sorrow and grief over the broken dreams we had for our future, learned He is enough. Paul wrote about this learning in his letter to the Philippians.

Not that I am speaking of being in need, for *I have learned* in whatever situation I am in to be content. I know how to be brought low, and I know how to abound. In any and every circumstance, *I have learned* the secret of facing plenty and hunger, abundance and need. I can do all things through him who strengthens me.

Philippians 4:11–13, emphasis added

Paul spoke of abundance and need—and being content in either. I imagine your daughter is a lot like mine and has a limited understanding of need. Casiday has everything she needs and a great deal of what she wants. And yet, she struggles to be content. Like little Sarah, her eyes are often focused on what she doesn't have. So how do we help our girls (and ourselves) learn to be content?

Grasping Gratitude

A few years ago I read *Let Hope In* by Pete Wilson. It is one of my all-time favorites, and I've underlined and scribbled in the margins every time I've re-read it. One sentence in the chapter titled "Showing Gratitude" resonated within me and continues to challenge me: "I'm learning we can't be grateful for something we feel entitled to, even if it's as simple as a phone or other technology."[1] Ouch, huh? At the bottom of the page I wrote, "How does this truth change the way I should parent? Am I raising an entitled child, or a grateful child?"

It's hard to be content with what we have and where we are when we feel entitled to something more. But when we choose to be grateful, everything changes. Kristen Welch speaks to this truth in her book *Raising Grateful Kids in an Entitled World*. She writes, "Nothing makes us more grateful than perspective."[2] Perspective. It's a great teacher, right? When we give our girls the opportunity to see how others live—both those with more and those with less—we can help them begin to learn about gratitude and the truth James expressed. "Every good gift and every perfect gift is from above, coming down from the Father of lights, with whom there is no variation or shadow due to change" (James 1:17).

Recognizing that all they have is due to God's goodness—not their worthiness or accomplishment—helps our girls learn, as Paul did, to be content in all things—not through our strength, but through His.

PRAYERS

Lord, I pray _____ will always find her greatest treasure is You. May she not be distracted and swayed by the things of this world, but may her heart find full contentment in You alone. (Matthew 6:21)

Lord, in her life, _____ will undoubtedly face seasons of abundance and times of need. My prayer for her is that she would always recognize that in You she can be satisfied and content regardless of her circumstances and situation. (Philippians 4:10–13)

Lord, may _____ always delight herself in You. When the enemy whispers that You are holding back good things from her, may she be firmly rooted in the truth of Your love and care. (Psalm 37:4)

Lord, I pray _____ will be grateful! May her life be marked by the ready acknowledgment that everything she has is a gift from You. (James 1:17)

Lord, there may be days when _____ looks around and wishes her life were different. I pray she won't stay there in discontent, but rather that she will live well the life You have assigned her. May she be satisfied with the purpose You have given her. (1 Corinthians 7:17)

Lord, I pray _____ will know You have "dealt bountifully" with her. Even when her circumstances aren't what she expected or even hoped for, may she see Your hand at work and be content in the path You have laid for her. (Psalm 13:6)

Lord, may _____ find her deepest satisfaction in You. May she rejoice in the love You have for her and find gladness in what You offer her. (Psalm 90:14)

Lord, You say those who hunger and thirst for righteousness will know the fullness of being satisfied in You. I pray _____ will find her truest contentment in pursuing You. (Matthew 5:6)

Lord, the day may come when _____ is weary. She may feel as though she has no hope. I pray that if she ever finds herself there, she will remember that You desire to satisfy her. May she know the contentment of walking with You every day, experiencing the countless ways You replenish and restore our souls. (Jeremiah 31:25)

Lord, I pray _____ will know the fullness of life You offer! As she abides in You, may she be content and find rest and satisfaction, regardless of her circumstances. (Proverbs 19:23)

Just for Moms

I shared about being told we'd never have a child and how God used the lyrics of a song to whisper His love and care to our broken hearts. In July 1999, just four months after that hard doctor's appointment in Birmingham, we found out I was pregnant with Casiday. We chose Hope for her middle name as a reminder of our journey, a way to recall the faithfulness of God even in the hardest days of our lives. We prayed for more children. We never planned on raising an only child, but when we chose to trust God's plan for our family, we made a decision to be content with His will for our lives.

There have been times when I've forgotten to be grateful for the one child we have, and have had to wrestle through my desire for more. I'm still learning what contentment is in many areas of my life. Maybe you are also? It isn't just our girls who look around and want something more or different. We have those same pangs of dissatisfaction. But just as our daughters can learn to be content and choose gratitude, so can we.

Lord, it's hard to be content sometimes. We get distracted by what others have (or seem to have) and lose sight of the gifts You have generously poured out in our lives. We need You to meet us right in the middle of our longings and desires for something different. Help us to see the beauty in our lives just as they are. Teach us to choose gratitude, even when our circumstances feel overwhelming. Help us trust Your plan, even when our lives are nothing like we'd planned. May we delight ourselves in You. May our hearts' treasure be found in You alone. And as we learn contentment, may we model it for our daughters. In Jesus' name, Amen.

Girl Talk

For little girls—Gather up all her toys and put them in one spot. As you remove one toy at a time from the pile, ask her if she still has enough to play with. Talk with her about being content and realizing how much she has. Pray with her about having a grateful heart.

For "middle" girls—Ask your girl what possession she treasures most. Talk about why it's precious to her and how it makes her feel to have it. Tell her about something you treasure and why. Share Matthew 6:21 with her and discuss what it means that our heart is where our treasure is. This might be a good time to tell her about a time you thought some thing or some relationship would make you content and how ultimately it didn't. Remind her our true treasure is Jesus, and He wants us to be content in Him alone.

For older girls—Head to the mall with your girl. As you wander through the stores, ask her to show you what she'd buy for herself if money were no object. (Again, a reminder not to judge her choices! You want her to feel free to be honest with you.) Take some pictures of her trying things on. When you get home, talk with her about the difference between what she looked at in the mall and what is hanging in her closet. Ask her if looking at what she has is more depressing after seeing all the fun stuff at the mall. Read Philippians 4:10–13 with her. Highlight the word *learned* and share with her how you are learning to be content no matter what your circumstances. Be honest with her about how you struggle in this area and ask her to pray for you. Give her an opportunity to share about her own discontentment, and pray with her.

9

Undivided

May she love God with an undivided heart.

I will give thanks to you, O Lord my God, with my whole heart,
and I will glorify your name forever.

Psalm 86:12

I love you with my whoooooooooole heart!" four-year-old
Rebecca said dramatically as she wrapped her arms around
her mom.

Her mom grinned and scooped up her daughter saying, "I
love you too!"

Right about that time, the little girl's daddy rounded the
corner. When she saw him, Rebecca squirmed loose from her
mother's hold and called out, "Daddy! Daddy! I've been waiting for you aallllll morning!"

Her mom looked at me and said, "Well, I guess we know
who her heart belongs to, right?" I laughed with her as I handed

over the bag her daughter had brought to the preschool class that Sunday morning.

I imagine Rebecca's mom isn't the only one of us girl moms who understands what it is to be second fiddle in the eyes of a daddy's girl. And I'd wager that at least a few of you reading were daddy's girls yourselves. (I definitely was. And honestly, still am.)

As Casiday has grown up, I have found great joy in watching her relationship with Scott grow and flourish. I am thankful they enjoy many of the same types of music and movies. Few things bring a bigger smile to my face than listening to them laugh together about an online video I don't find humorous at all. I love that she wants to spend time with him.

But even more than the love she has for her daddy, I pray she will have a wholehearted love for the Lord.

An Undivided Heart

We all live with divided hearts. We love our parents and our children and our husbands and our friends. We give pieces of ourselves to everyone. (Sometimes until there are no pieces left. Can I get an amen?) So what did Jesus mean when He said,

> The most important is, "Hear, O Israel: The Lord our God, the Lord is one. And you shall love the Lord your God with all your heart and with all your soul and with all your mind and with all your strength." The second is this: "You shall love your neighbor as yourself." There is no other commandment greater than these.

> Mark 12:29–31

How do we love God with our whole hearts and still have love to give to others? The answer is this: We can only love others when we know the love of God.

Consider John's words, "Beloved, let us love one another, for love is from God, and whoever loves has been born of God and knows God" (1 John 4:7). God's love in us empowers us to love others. This is why we give Him our whole hearts. If we don't, we will never be able to love Him and love others.

Five Ways to Live with a Heart Wholly Devoted to God

Worship

One thing have I asked of the Lord, that will I seek after: that I may dwell in the house of the Lord all the days of my life.

Psalm 27:4

Let's start with the most obvious: An undivided heart worships. This isn't about attending church or liking a particular style of music; worship is about attributing worth to something or Someone. David was essentially saying he wanted to spend his life in the presence of God. Paul spoke of this when he urged the Romans to present themselves as living sacrifices. He called it their "spiritual worship" (Romans 12:1). When we realize our whole lives are an act of worship, we see how everything we do and say points to the Lord. And it is our job as moms to help our girls learn the same lesson.

Heed

And he said to them, "Follow me, and I will make you fishers of men." Immediately they left their nets and followed him.

Matthew 4:19–20

Immediately. These fishers of fish left their nets as soon as Jesus invited them. They walked away from torn nets and fishy odors and chose to follow a dusty rabbi. They heard the call, and they heeded it. Sometimes we hear the call and then we wait for God to show us photo ID. We want to be sure it will all work out the way we plan. A wholehearted disciple will follow immediately, trusting the words of the One who has always been faithful. Even when it doesn't make sense. Maybe especially when it doesn't make sense. Let's be moms who show our girls how to heed the voice of Christ.

Offer

Through him then let us continually offer up a sacrifice of praise to God, that is, the fruit of lips that acknowledge his name.

Hebrews 13:15

Time and again we see the men and women of Scripture praising God. From Genesis to Revelation, the Bible is replete with examples of the "sacrifice of praise." From Noah leaving the ark (Genesis 8:20) to the worship service in heaven (Revelation 22:3), we find the offerings of His people. The prophets praised Him during the darkest days (Habakkuk 3:18–19). Job praised Him in his suffering (Job 1:21). The early church praised Him as they saw Him work in and through them (Acts 2:46–47). Paul and Silas praised Him from prison (Acts 16:25).

Now it's our turn, moms. We offer our "sacrifice of praise" and we teach our girls to do the same. We help them remember God is good and we can trust Him in every situation we face. And as we do, we see that the offering continues on.

Linger

But one thing is necessary. Mary has chosen the good portion, which will not be taken away from her.

Luke 10:42

Mary chose to linger near Jesus while Martha was hustling in the kitchen. We might call her lazy, but Jesus said she'd chosen what was necessary. Some days it can be hard to linger in the presence of Jesus. We're sleep deprived or stressed out. The kids are out of school. Someone is sick. The dog is puking. Our attention gets moved from lingering to hustling. Here's what I know: The hustle won't ever make room for the lingering. But when we linger, the hustle isn't as stressful.

Our girls are watching every move we make. They are taking note of how we manage stress and where we give our time and effort. Let's show them the importance and value of lingering in the presence of the Lord.

Embrace

I will give thanks to you, O Lord my God, with my whole heart, and I will glorify your name forever.

Psalm 86:12

Gratitude and glory. That's what we give God in return for all He has done for us. We embrace Him wholly, knowing that without Him we truly have nothing. Paul spoke to this when he wrote, "Indeed, I count everything as loss because of the surpassing worth of knowing Christ Jesus my Lord" (Philippians 3:8). Nothing matters outside of Him. Nothing.

How well are we doing at showing our girls what it is to embrace a wholehearted devotion to the Lord? Are they seeing in us a consistent pattern of giving thanks and glory to Him? If we don't teach them, who will?

Living with an undivided heart isn't easy. As long as we are here on earth, we will be torn between flesh and spirit. Jesus spoke of it to the disciples in the garden (Mark 14:38), and Paul wrote of the depth of the struggle he faced.

For I know that nothing good dwells in me, that is, in my flesh. For I have the desire to do what is right, but not the ability to carry it out. For I do not do the good I want, but the evil I do not want is what I keep on doing.

Romans 7:18–19

Here's the challenge to us as moms: to pursue life with an undivided heart, recognizing our need for Christ to work it out in us. And to invite our girls to join us in the pursuit.

PRAYERS

Lord, I pray _____'s heart will be wholly devoted to You. May she know the joy and peace of loving You with all her heart, all her soul, and all her strength. (Deuteronomy 6:5)

Lord, may _____ count everything else as worthless when compared to knowing You! If she suffers, if she celebrates, if she's hurting, if she's happy, whatever she loses, may it all pale when it stands next to knowing You and the fullness of Your love for her. (Philippians 3:8)

Lord, in a world where love is transient, may _____ _____ recognize Your love is permanent. And may the love You offer be the place she stakes her life. May she desire You far more than she longs for anything this world affords. (1 John 2:15)

Lord, just as the disciples walked away from everything they knew, everything their lives had been built upon, may _____ choose to follow You with abandon, without hesitation. May she be ready to leave behind everything in order to walk with You. (Matthew 4:19–20)

Lord, I pray _____ will, like Mary, choose the better part. May her heart's desire be to sit at Your feet and to know You more and more. (Luke 10:42)

Lord, may _____'s whole heart be committed to You. May she obey Your commands and love Your Word. When she questions what to do, may her heart lead her to You. (Psalm 119:145)

Lord, in an increasingly ungrateful world, may _____ _____ give thanks to You with her whole heart. May she look for ways to praise You, to give glory to Your name. (Psalm 86:12)

Lord, the sacrifice You desire is always our hearts. I pray _____ will continually offer You her praise. May she see Your work in, around, and through her. May she praise You for who You are and all You do. (Hebrews 13:15)

Lord, as David prayed for one thing, to be in Your presence always, I pray _____ will have that same passionate desire to be where You are. May she know that You are the only thing that matters and be committed to seeking You with all she is and all she has for all her days. (Psalm 27:4)

Lord, may _____ have a steadfast heart. Just as Your heart is always bent toward us, may hers be bent toward You. May the song of her life be one of undivided devotion to You. (Psalm 57:7)

Just for Moms

I know, this chapter was hard. It was hard to write, because I always feel torn. No matter how much I want to give to the Lord, I keep running into obstacles. You know, like laundry and life. I want to get up early so I have more time to study, but we get to bed late and I figure a mom with enough sleep is better for everyone.

It comes down to this: Will I choose to be grateful and give Him glory? Or will I choose to be grumpy and give everyone griping? If we want to live wholeheartedly for the Lord, we will determine to choose gratitude and glory even when we don't feel like it or really want to.

Lord, we're tired. And we're torn in a million directions. Some days we can barely remember our own names. So here we are, empty and in desperate need of You. We long for undivided hearts, to desire You above anything else. Thank You for meeting us where we are, for giving us grace in the middle of all the chaos. Will you help us be mindful to praise Your name even in the messiness of our daily lives? Help us choose the better part, the one necessary thing—help us choose You. And as we choose You, may our children learn to do the same. In Jesus' name, Amen.

Girl Talk

For little girls—Look through a photo album with your daughter. As you look at the pictures, talk about who is in them and why they are special to you. Ask her to name some people she loves. Read 1 John 4:7 with her and talk with her about how God's love for us is what helps us love others.

For "middle" girls—Ask your girl if there has ever been a time when she felt like God was telling her to do something. It may have been when she made a profession of faith. Or it could be when she felt like He was leading her to be kind to someone. Read Matthew 4:18–21 with her. Talk with her about how the men immediately followed Jesus. Ask her if she was quick to obey when she felt the Lord telling her to do something. Discuss with her how important it is for us to listen carefully for the Lord's voice and then to do what He says quickly.

For big girls—Set aside some time to spend with your girl. Ask her about what is difficult for her right now. Maybe it's a friendship or a class at school. Whatever it is, discuss with her why it's hard and how she is managing the difficulty. Read Psalm 86:12 with her. Ask her how she can give thanks to God even in the middle of the hard days. Pray with her for wisdom and grace to trust God in the situations she shared.

PART 3

Prayers for Her Mind

M any of the most difficult battles our girls will face are battles of the mind. Overcoming negative or untrue thought patterns can take a lifetime. Our prayers can be a wall for them, a barrier to keep those dangerous thoughts from taking root in our girls' minds.

These next chapters will help us understand the necessity of having minds stayed in God's Word. We pray for them to have sound minds, rooted in truth and knowledge. We lay a solid foundation for them to walk in the full peace and hope they have in Christ.

10

Stayed

May she set her mind on the things of God.

Set your minds on things that are above, not on things that are on earth.

Colossians 3:2

"Stay right there!" my friend Lori firmly said to her eight-year-old daughter.

"It's okay, Mommy, I can do this."

"Missy, I said stay there."

And then, as if in slow motion, we watched Missy lose her footing on the jungle gym and fall to the hard playground surface. As my friend rushed to her daughter, the high-pitched screams of a terrified child rang out.

Fifteen minutes later, Missy was back on the playground. Shaken up and scared, but otherwise just fine, she was happily pumping her legs to go higher on the swing. My friend looked from her daughter to me and, with a deep sigh, said, "I told her to stay where she was. I don't know why she doesn't listen to me. I knew she'd fall. She could have been seriously hurt."

"I know. Why can't our kids understand we just want to protect them from unnecessary hurt?" I commiserated.

Lori wasn't trying to keep Missy from having fun. Her instruction wasn't meant as an insult to Missy's ability to balance herself on the jungle gym. She knew Missy's limits. She understood that if Missy's attention was diverted from staying balanced and holding on, the girl would fall. Her mom wanted to protect her.

Just like Lori knew the risks of Missy's diverted attention, our heavenly Father understands how dangerous it is for us to have our focus shift from Him to anything else.

Stay Focused

When Paul admonished the Colossians to "set [their] minds on things that are above" (Colossians 3:2), it was a call to stay focused. He was reminding them of the necessity of keeping their minds centered on Christ. He knew if they allowed themselves to get distracted by all the stuff of the world, they would forget who they were in Christ.

And the same is true for us and for our girls.

When we focus on things that are above, we are essentially setting our gaze on two very important things.

Exalted Savior

We know Christ is now in heaven (Acts 1:9), seated at the right hand of God (Mark 16:19), ever interceding on our behalf (Hebrews 7:25). When we stay focused on Jesus, we are

86

reminded of who we are in Him, of our privileged status as coheirs (Romans 8:17), more than conquerors (Romans 8:37), and redeemed through His blood (Revelation 5:9). Knowing who He is and who we are in Him keeps us focused on pressing on toward the goal (Philippians 3:14).

Eternal Hope

Because of Christ, because we belong to Him, we have eternal hope. We set our gaze toward Him, even in the middle of our earthly struggles and heartaches. Our girls need to hear us tell them this truth. When they face mean girls at school, we need to remind them this life isn't all there is. We point them to the unwavering hope we have in Christ (Hebrews 6:19). Not only are we overcomers now, but we have the assurance of eternal victory in Christ (1 Corinthians 15:57).

Resetting to Whatever

How do we stay focused? How do we keep our gaze on our Savior and our hope? Let's face it, that really is the hard part. When everything is chaos or the crisis hits, how do we move our focus from our circumstances to our confidence in Him? How do we align our focus with our faith?

One word: whatever.

Take a moment to read Philippians 4:8–9. Even if you already know what it says, go ahead and look it up and read it.

It's good, right? I feel like Paul was writing with great intensity when he got to this part of his letter to the Philippian church. The cadence and rhythm of these verses is powerful, but the words—wow. The words are even more so. Paul gives us the key to resetting our focus, to resetting our minds. Think about *whatever*.

Whatever is true. How often are the thoughts wandering through our minds and the minds of our girls untrue? The first and vital step to resetting our gaze on things above is to focus on truth. Who He is, who I am in Him, what He has said, what He has promised.

Whatever is honorable. I know I can think less-than-honorable thoughts, things I would never want someone else to know. When these thoughts wiggle their way into my mind, I have two choices: invite them in for a lingering conversation or escort them to the door and shut it firmly with them on the outside. Our girls have these same options.

Whatever is just. This one is tricky. We tend to think in terms of what seems just or fair to us. But Paul urges us to measure our thoughts according to what God says is just. We need to call the sin in our minds and hearts exactly what it is and deal with it accordingly. And we must encourage our girls to do the same.

Whatever is pure. I've talked to Casiday a lot about this one. When we allow impurity into our minds through what we watch or listen to, we make it harder to keep focused on Christ and to reset ourselves when necessary. Our girls need us to help them make decisions about what to let in, using purity as a standard.

Whatever is lovely. I like lovely things. But sometimes I get so busy I forget to stop and savor the beauty around me. We need to teach our girls to see and think about the good things around them, those good gifts God gives us (James 1:17).

Whatever is commendable. I was sharing these verses with some college girls, and I told them this basically means, "Be nice!" Keep your mind focused on what is commendable about others, about situations, and even about yourself. The world is full of critics. We need to be encouragers.

Whatever is excellent. Sometimes we get focused on what's going wrong, what's a mess. It happened the other day with

Casiday. She got her first paycheck from her first job. She was thrilled—until she starting thinking others may be making more money than she is. We quickly reminded her how happy she had been to get that job and how much she was enjoying it. We must choose to see what's excellent.

Whatever is worthy of praise. Again, plenty of people love to be the critic. We can reset our own minds but also offer a powerful testimony when we choose to think and speak about what is praiseworthy.

That day on the playground, Missy eased her way back toward the jungle gym. Sneaking glances our way to see if her mom was watching, Missy slowly put one hand, then the other, one foot, and then the other on the metal bars. I nudged Lori, who simply looked up at Missy and said, "Do you want to fall again?" Missy shook her head and slowly climbed back down.

Sometimes we just need to reset our focus.

PRAYERS

Lord, just as You command us to love You with all our hearts, You also want our whole minds as well. I pray _____ will realize her faith is a matter of her mind as well as her heart. May she fill her mind with the truth of who You are and Your plan for her. (Mark 12:30)

Lord, sometimes our minds get lost in what has already happened, the things we can't change. When _____ _____ gets into that cycle, I pray You will draw her out, reminding her to forget what is behind and press toward what is ahead. May she remember the goal is You, only You. (Philippians 3:13–14)

Lord, Your Word says, "As we think, so we are" (Proverbs 23:7). May _____ think on the things that are worthy of You: the pure and beautiful, the noble and excellent, those things worthy of praise. May her mind be set on the excellent things of You. (Philippians 4:8–9)

Lord, I pray _____'s mind will be set on the things of the Spirit, not on things of the flesh. May her focus be the life and peace You offer. May the bright lights of this world not distract her, but rather may she aim her sight on the true Light we have in You. (Romans 8:5–6)

Lord, all around _____ are the attractions and temptations the world offers. I pray she will set her mind on You, and as she does, may she find her greatest joy and satisfaction in what You hold dear. (Colossians 3:2)

Lord, in a world full of chaos and confusion, I pray _____ will know the peace of having her mind stayed on You. May she learn to trust in You always, knowing You keep her safe in body, heart, and mind. (Isaiah 26:3)

Lord, I pray _____ will not forget how good You are. May she recount the good things You have done for her and remember that You are her hope. (Psalm 78:7)

Lord, may _____ meditate on Your Word, may it fill her mind and dwell in her heart. As she fixes her thoughts on You and learns to love Your commands, I pray she will also find deep peace and comfort in the knowledge of Your care for her. (Psalm 119:15)

Lord, just as David asked You to test His thoughts, I pray
You will examine _____ 's heart and mind.
Reveal to her anything that doesn't please You and give
her courage to follow where You lead. (Psalm 139:23–24)

Lord, Your Word tests us and trains us. May _____
_____ allow Scripture to guide her thoughts, to lead
her actions, and to convict her of sin. May she be certain
of the truth Your Word contains and build her life upon
it. (2 Timothy 3:16)

Just for Moms

Some days when I'm watching the news or just thinking about
all the sorrow, suffering, and sin in our world, I realize how easy
it is to shift my focus from hope to despair. I have to stop and
remind myself of God's goodness and His sovereignty. Often
I turn to Hebrews 11 as a way of resetting my mind on the
ways God has always been faithful. This chapter also helps me
remember I'm not alone—that "great cloud of witnesses" has
traveled these dusty roads before me (Hebrews 12:1).

When you are overwhelmed by all the heartache and you feel
helpless and even hopeless, reset your mind on the truth we
find in God's Word. For me, reading about Moses and Rahab
and others who have suffered and endured reminds me of the
true hope I have in Christ, setting my mind on the promise of
eternity with Him.

*Some days are just hard, Lord. You know the anguish
of this earth, the hard hearts, and the anxious minds. In
our fears and frustrations, we often fail to stay focused
on You. We need You to give us wisdom to see the eternal hope in the middle of everyday chaos. May we be*

reminded of Your goodness and faithfulness when we're overwhelmed. When our minds are full of undone tasks and unmet expectations, I pray You will speak peace and truth over us. May we find solace in the certainty of Your Word and allow our thoughts to dwell on things that are true and noble and excellent. When we're tempted to give in to despair, may we choose to set our minds on You. In Jesus' name, Amen.

Girl Talk

For little girls—Remember playing the memory game as a child? This game is a great way to help your daughter begin to understand how easily she can be distracted. Play the game with her and explain that just like we focus to remember where the matching cards are, we also need to focus to remember how much God loves us and cares for us.

For "middle" girls—Ask your daughter what she daydreams about, and what she's doing or where she is when she finds herself daydreaming. Share a time when you were daydreaming and needed to pay attention. Talk with her about learning to reset her mind and focus on the Lord when she finds herself distracted by people or situations around her.

For big girls—Ask your daughter to play a few of her favorite songs for you. Talk with her about the messages in the songs she chose. Discuss whether they reflect God's desires for us or not. Encourage her to use Philippians 4:8–9 as a standard for her life.

Renewed

May she seek to have her mind renewed by God.

And to be renewed in the spirit of your minds, and to put on the new self, created after the likeness of God in true righteousness and holiness.

Ephesians 4:23–24

Every morning, I move, bleary-eyed and stumbling, from my bedroom to the kitchen, where Scott (because he wakes up way before me) already has the coffee brewed. I slowly pour the liquid gold into my favorite mug—a heavy white one with a vintage typewriter and the word "Writer" on it. I add a little bit of cane sugar and just enough creamer to create the perfect blend of sweet and creamy. I move from there to the coral upholstered chair that sits in my office and, as I sit down, I take my first sip. Clearly, coffee is an important part of my day.

In our home there are no fewer than six ways to make coffee. We have everything from your basic coffeepot to a French press. But, hands down, the best coffee is from a percolator. Remember those? We have both an electric one and one used on the stove. You put the water in and it bubbles up through the coffee grounds. You can hear it as it percolates. I love that sound, the bubbling and the popping. Since it takes longer to percolate coffee than it does to brew it in the coffeepot, we don't use ours all the time. But when we do, it's the smoothest coffee we ever make—definitely worth the extra time.

As a little girl, I faithfully memorized my Bible verses for Sunday school and Vacation Bible school. I earned gold stars and received awards. I'd study the words and repeat them time and again so I could recite them perfectly for my teachers. But, if I'm honest, I know very few of those verses today. The process was sort of like using my Keurig—quick and effective. I love my Keurig. I am thankful to be able to make a cup of coffee in just a couple of minutes, because some days that is all I have.

But Scott and I quickly found the Keurig doesn't work for us every day. It wasn't a good investment because we drink too much coffee. Those little cups got expensive quickly.

Renewed minds are like percolated coffee. It's a slower process than simply memorizing Scripture. The Word, like the water in the percolator, moves through our minds, touching each thought, desire, and dream. But it takes time for this to happen. It's an investment of more than just a few minutes every day for an immediate reward.

We live in an instant-gratification world. The truth is, a lot of people who love coffee don't even make their own. They just head to their favorite coffee shop and order what they want. They never learn the process of making a latte or an Americano.

This is the world our girls are being raised in, a world where memorizing Scripture seems unnecessary. They don't have to know where verses are or even the full wording; they just need a phrase that's close so they can do an Internet search.

Of course, I also enjoy the way technology has made searching Scripture much easier. I relied on the quick searching power of my computer as I waded through countless verses for the two hundred prayers in this book.

But when it comes to having the mind of Christ—a mind set on the things above, a mind renewed by Him—there is no substitute for allowing Scripture to percolate in us.

So how do we teach our girls to do this? What do we say to them about this process? Or maybe you're thinking, *How am I supposed to do this myself?* Ahh, now it's time for the fun part.

Percolate and Permeate

Percolate can mean "to show activity, movement, or life; grow or spread gradually; germinate."[1] We want the Word to show activity in our lives. Learning Scripture and allowing it to renew our minds is a lifelong process. Because the Word is living and active (Hebrews 4:12), we find its truth can often be multi-layered, and the meaning and application deepens as we mature in our faith.

When we talk to our girls about learning the Word, we need to remind them it is more than simply memorizing Bible verses. Part of our job is to help them realize this is a discipline they will need to pursue for their whole lives.

And they need to see us doing it too!

Just as we want to let the Word percolate inside us, we also need to allow Scripture to permeate our minds and hearts.

My mom hates the smell of coffee. I mean, she seriously hates it. (Yes, it remains unclear to me how it's possible that I am hers.) She says it makes the whole house stink. I say it makes the whole house smell amazing. But here's what we agree on: The smell of coffee saturates the space it's in.

When we allow the Word to percolate inside our mind, it saturates every part of us.

I've often told people the reason I pray Scripture is because Scripture is what I know. My prayers are guided by the time I've spent in study and meditation.

But How?

You're probably right here with me, nodding your head and thinking, *I know this is all true.* But it's also possible you've had another thought right alongside it, something like, *Yeah, but T. L. is a Bible teacher. She studies all the time and it probably comes easily to her. I'm not like that at all.*

Yeah, well, let me assure you, I'm just a girl. A girl who loves the Word of God, but also a girl who has the same temptation to hit the snooze, to binge on Netflix, or to overschedule my life and find out I have left little space for things like meditation and soaking in the Word.

Over the years, I've found there are a few simple ways I can keep myself on track in this area. I've shared them with countless women, most of whom have found at least one or two ways that also work for them, even if they need a little bit of tweaking to fit their unique situations.

Read. It sounds incredibly basic, I know. But I've learned that there are a whole lot of women who don't regularly read the Bible. It has nothing to do with not wanting to read Scripture or believing it isn't valuable. It has to do with actually sitting down and doing it. Here is where technology is totally our friend—we can listen to Scripture on our phones while we do dishes, nurse a baby, or drive to work.

Rewind. I'm notorious for rewinding when we're watching a movie. If I miss something or don't understand what happened, I hit the button and watch again. I also do this with Scripture. If I am reading a passage and it doesn't make sense, I go back a little farther. I've learned that reading the verses or even chapters around what I'm studying help give me the context I need to make sense of what I'm studying.

Reflect. I give myself space to reflect on what I'm learning. Which means I don't go from one Bible study to the next with no time in between. In fact, the deeper I've studied, the more time I give myself to reflect on what I've learned before I jump into the next study. For example, I once did an in-depth study of the Gospel of John. It was a great study, but I wanted time to reflect on what I'd learned, to reexamine some of the passages we'd read, and to allow it all to sink in before I started another study. From me to you, it's okay to give ourselves time to reflect. I often use Saturday mornings for reflecting on what I've read and studied over the week.

Repeat. One of my favorite ways to dig deep into a passage or book is simply to read it over and over. For me, this works best with shorter books like Philippians or Ruth. Repetition is a great way to let the Word sink deep into our hearts and minds.

Restart. Let's be honest here, sometimes this is where we are. We've gotten off track for whatever reason and we don't need guilt. We just need to pick up our Bibles and restart.

When we are faithful to invest time in learning the Word and to allow our minds to be renewed and shaped by what we read, our girls will learn from our example.

And here's what I've learned, whether my coffee is percolated, brewed, or fixed in my Keurig, it is always good. So on the days when you have lots of time to let the Word simmer and soak in deep, cherish it. And when you are in a grab-and-go season, trust the sufficiency of the Word to meet you where you are and accomplish what God intends. And for the days in between (which are really most of our days), savor the Word and allow your mind to be renewed by the truth God offers. And invite your daughter to grow in those same habits.

PRAYERS

Lord, in a culture that esteems conformity, may _____ _____ choose to be transformed into Your image. May she seek the renewal of mind You offer so that she will be able to understand and live in Your will for her. (Romans 12:2)

Lord, I pray _____ ' s mind will be renewed by Your Spirit. As she grows and matures, may she desire to be more like You. May she cherish being created in Your likeness, seeking Your righteousness in all ways. (Ephesians 4:23–24)

Lord, You say that when we belong to You we are new creations! May _____ allow that truth to be centered in her mind so that she can walk in the new life You offer to those who belong to You. (2 Corinthians 5:17)

Lord, I pray _____ will have the mind of Christ. May her thoughts and actions be rooted in the same humility and love as Christ's, that others may see Him in her at all times. (1 Corinthians 2:16)

Lord, I pray You will put Your Word deep inside _____ _____. Write it on her heart, embed it in her mind. I pray she will know the beauty of being Yours, of knowing You are her God. (Hebrews 8:10)

Lord, Your requirements are few, but they demand much from us. I pray _____ will always heed the desires You have for her, that she will live justly, love mercy, and walk humbly with You. (Micah 6:8)

Lord, I pray _____ will have the wisdom that comes from You, that she will hold You in high regard and recognize Your holiness. May she have deep insight, an awareness that can only come from Your Spirit at work in her. (Proverbs 9:10)

Lord, I know You have a great plan for _____, and I pray she will live under the umbrella of Your protection. May she walk in confidence, knowing she has been made new in You. I pray her mind will be continually renewed by her pursuit of You. (Colossians 3:10)

Lord, I pray _____ will walk in the truth of Your Word. May she be certain of Your steadfast love for her and may she live aligned with the truth of Scripture. As she grows in knowledge, may her mind be focused on You. (Psalm 119:88)

Lord, it's easy for us to start thinking we are good, especially when we compare ourselves with others. But the truth is, there is nothing good in us. May _____ grasp that anything good others see in her is entirely You at work in her. (Romans 7:23)

Just for Moms

As much as I enjoy coffee, lately I've developed an affinity for a cup of tea in the afternoon. Around 3:30 or 4:00, I make my way to the kitchen and set the teapot on the stove. While I wait for the whistling, I choose which type of tea I want. Most often lately, I've been selecting Earl Grey with just a bit of honey and a splash of cream. I usually add a cookie or something sweet and settle into that same chair in my office where I study and write.

Often during this time I read a devotional or a Psalm—just a small way to reset my heart and mind before the chaos of our evening begins. Maybe I need to add that to my list of Rs—reset. Because some days that is exactly what we need, right? Maybe today you need a reset. I totally understand.

Lord, You see our hearts and know how much we want to spend time in the Word. You know the thoughts of our minds and recognize how much we want to be centered on You. But You also know the never-ending lists of things to be done, people to be loved, places to be. Will You help us recognize when we need a reset? Will You bring to mind a familiar verse, a reminder of how much You love and care for us? You are kind and generous to meet us right where we are. Thank You for that. Renew our minds, and fill us with the truth of Your love and peace. Grant us the strength we need, through You, to do the things that must be done. And may we dwell richly in Your Word, allowing it to percolate and permeate every part of our minds, our hearts, and our lives. In Jesus' name, Amen.

Girl Talk

For little girls—Ask your daughter what her favorite Bible story is. If she can't think of one, tell her one of your favorites. Talk with her about the value of reading the Bible and learning from it. Let her help you find her favorite story in the Bible and then read it together.

For "middle" girls—Just as suggested for little girls, talk with your daughter about her favorite Bible story or verse. Look it up together and talk about it. This is a great time to share with your girl a passage or verse that is especially meaningful to you right now.

For big girls—As our girls get older, it is important that we help them understand the value of time spent in Bible study. But they also need to be reminded this isn't a quest for perfection. Talk with your daughter about what your quiet time looks like and how it's changed at different times in your life. Share the five Rs from this chapter with her and be sure to remind her that if she has gotten off track, she can restart.

12

Guarded

May she trust God to guard her mind.

I have stored up your word in my heart, that I might not sin against you.

Psalm 119:11

Opening the envelope and pulling out the card, I couldn't stop the tears from falling. Paulee, my eight-year-old niece, had carefully and beautifully written out John 1:3: "All things were made through him, and without him was not any thing made that was made." I called my sister-in-law to let her know I'd received the card, and she told me Paulee had spent hours working on the lettering for the verse and coloring the picture she drew next to it. "She chose it from the list of verses you sent her in your last letter," Beth said.

She's my "mini me," her mom and I always say. She loves all things girly and sparkly, believes every day is better with cake, and this little girl is serious about the Word of God. Paulee and I have always had a special bond, which I suppose is not altogether uncommon with nieces and aunts. But it's our shared love for Scripture that gives me the greatest joy.

From the day she first professed her faith in Christ when she was six, this little girl has recognized the beauty and value of time spent in the Bible. Beth wrote a blog post sharing Paulee's salvation story, and my favorite part is this:

> She told me that the next thing she needed to do would be to "get baptized." Because that is what Jesus did. And she wants to be just like Jesus. But since she has to wait for that, she needed to find a Bible to read. Because if she is going to act like Jesus, and be like Jesus, she probably should read about what he did and how he acted.[1]

Sweet story, huh? She's a precious child, this little niece of mine. And since she was saved, Paulee has continued to study and learn Scripture. She's been teaching her younger sisters how to have a quiet time and often takes time to read the Bible to them and share her notes for them to carefully copy.

Whenever I look at the card on my desk or read one of Beth's Facebook posts about Paulee's journals full of Scripture she has carefully copied, Psalm 119:11 always comes to mind: "I have stored up your word in my heart, that I might not sin against you." Paulee, better than many of us, recognizes the importance of loving Scripture.

How can we be more like this little girl? And how can we help our own girls learn to love the Bible and understand how God's Word guards our hearts and minds?

Whenever I am asked to teach or share about the significance of the Word, I always go to the same place—Psalm 119. This psalm of David, the longest chapter of the Bible, has a singular focus: the necessity of the Word in our lives.

Guarding Our Minds and Guiding Our Lives

The world says the Bible is just a dusty old book, nothing special, and certainly nothing to guide our lives by. As believers, though, we believe what the Word says about itself: It is God-breathed and useful, the sustenance for our souls. As moms, we must teach our girls not only the truth and value of Scripture but also the application and relevance of God's Word to our lives.

In Psalm 119, we find four specific ways the Bible guards our minds and guides our lives.

Deliberate study guides us to obedience.

Oh that my ways may be steadfast
in keeping your statutes.
Psalm 119:5

The more time we invest in learning and understanding Scripture, the more we recognize the path of obedience in our Christian lives. Verse 9 tells us that guarding ourselves with the Word is the only path to purity. In verse 60, the psalmist shares the urgency he feels to keep the Lord's commands. As we teach our girls to study the Word and pray for them to be focused students of Scripture, we lay a foundation for lifelong obedience.

Devotion to memorization provides us with protection.

I have stored up your word in my heart,
that I might not sin against you.
Psalm 119:11

Like me, you may have memorized this verse as a child. But also like me, you may struggle with regular memorization of Scripture. Challenge yourself and your daughter in this area. Verse 15 says, "I will meditate on your precepts and fix my eyes on your ways." We need to be focused on the Word, embedding it deep in our hearts and encouraging our girls to do the same. This is one of our most powerful tools for guarding our hearts against the schemes of our enemy.

Defining our lives by the truth of the Word gives us joy and peace.

> Your word is a lamp to my feet
> and a light to my path.
> Psalm 119:105

The prophet Amos said the Word of God is a plumb line for us, a tool to assess the alignment of our hearts with the righteousness of God's character (Amos 7:8). We conform ourselves to the unchangeable truth of Scripture. I love what the psalmist wrote in verse 111: "Your testimonies are my heritage forever, for they are the joy of my heart." Further, he writes in verse 165, "Great peace have those who love your law; nothing can make them stumble." When we allow God's Word to define our lives, we will experience the true joy, confidence, and peace He offers.

Disciplined time spent in Scripture guards our thoughts and actions.

> I rise before dawn and cry for help;
> I hope in your words.
> Psalm 119:147

Throughout this psalm, David writes of coming to the Lord throughout the day. I think it's easy for us to have our quiet times in the morning and never really give serious thought to the Word again during our days. But when we are disciplined about spending time in Scripture throughout the day, we are guarding ourselves with layers of protection.

I may be a tad bit biased, but I happen to think Paulee is a remarkable little girl. She's a beautiful illustration of coming to Christ like a child (Matthew 18:2). Her earnest desire to learn and grow and be obedient is both an inspiration and a challenge to me.

May we be moms who pray for our girls to seek the protection Scripture provides, to be disciplined to guard their minds and lives with the Word of God. And may we be moms who illustrate these practices in our own lives.

PRAYERS

Lord, I pray _____'s mind will be steadfast, disciplined in Your Word. May she be determined to obey the precepts You have given and immovable in her dedication to studying Scripture. (Psalm 119:5)

Lord, may _____ treasure the Bible. May she store up what she reads and learns and be quick to apply Your truth to the situations she faces in life. May she know, as Jesus modeled when He was tempted in the wilderness, it is Your Word that protects us against the enemy's lies and schemes. (Psalm 119:11)

Lord, _____ will need to understand how obeying Your Word protects her. Give her insight to grasp the path to follow You. (Psalm 119:27)

Lord, when afflictions come and she wonders how to proceed, I pray _____ will lean into the promise of life she has in You. May she go to You, rather than the things of the world, for comfort. (Psalm 119:50)

Lord, on the hard days, I pray _____ will learn to see You at work in her circumstances. May she recognize it is those times when she can comprehend the richness of Your Word and the depths of Your love. (Psalm 119:71)

Lord, I pray _____ will hope in Your Word. When life feels hopeless, I pray she will recall the hope she has in You. May the promises and truths she has read come quickly to her mind and help her reset her thoughts on You. (Psalm 119:81)

Lord, as _____ grows in You, may she comprehend the sweetness of Your Word. May she recognize how obedience and walking with You protect her heart and mind and guide her to the full life You have for her. (Psalm 119:103)

Lord, in a world full of darkness, may _____ find Your Word as her true light, a guide for navigating life. May she trust the truth of Scripture to lead her according to Your way. (Psalm 119:105)

Lord, the best way to protect us from the schemes of the enemy is to focus on the truth of Your Word. I pray _____ will be dedicated to turn to Scripture regularly. May time in the Bible not be a once-a-day habit but a throughout-the-day decision. (Psalm 119:164)

Lord, I pray _____ will be guided by Your Word. As she learns and applies the truths contained in Scripture, may she also be faithful to praise You for the way You provide for and protect her. (Psalm 119:175)

Just for Moms

Okay, let me be honest here. My daughter isn't like my niece. Though Casiday has been raised in a pastor's home, has grown up involved in church, and has seen both her parents be diligent in spiritual disciplines, she doesn't have that same fervent desire for writing Scripture and reading the Bible as Paulee does. One morning this week, when Casiday walked out the door for school, I realized it's been probably two weeks since she has sat across from me in the morning as we both read our devotions. And while morning devotions aren't a requirement of our faith, this practice of beginning the day with a few moments of reading Scripture and praying has been an ongoing part of my personal spiritual development. Because I've experienced the benefit of this practice in my life, I am committed to encouraging Casiday to make it a consistent aspect of her day as well. Certainly praying for my daughter isn't dependent on any time we may spend together in Bible reading, but it has been a sweet place for me to share with her what God is showing me, and it opens the door for her to ask questions and share her heart with me.

As Casiday rushed out the door that morning, the word *failure* immediately began ringing through my mind. Here I am, every single day, writing prayers and encouraging moms to pray earnestly and fervently for their girls . . . and me? Well, let's just say, some days the fruit of my ongoing prayers doesn't always seem evident.

The Prayers for Girls prayer that day was for our girls to be driven to grow in their faith (based on Ephesians 4:15). But when I read the verse, it was a whisper of grace. Y'all, we can't grow *for* our girls. We can't place that desire in their hearts. But we can pray! And we can set the example for them of faithfulness.

And we might also need to remember to look at our daughters' hearts for the fruit of Christ at work in them and not always measure it by quiet times, devotions, and that sort of thing. When I look at my girl and see the way she loves others and works hard and gives grace, I am reminded that this working out of our salvation (Philippians 2:12) looks different in each of us.

Lord, sometimes we hear about all the ways other peoples' kids are changing the world for You, and we feel like we're failing as moms. Will You use Your Word to guard our minds from these thoughts? Help us be diligent to soak up the truth and recognize it is You who does the work of guiding our girls to You and growing their faith. Remind us that we get to be an example for them, but the results are Your job, not ours. Give us wisdom to see where You are working and determination to keep praying no matter what! Also, God, help us follow Your lead and not compare ourselves or our kids to anyone else. You don't measure us by what another mom is doing, and we need not hold ourselves to that standard either. In Jesus' name, Amen.

Girl Talk

For little girls—Your daughter is never too young for you to begin memorizing Scripture with her. In fact, the earlier we start this practice, the better it is for our girls. One of the first verses Casiday learned was 1 John 4:8, "Anyone who does not love does not know God, because God is love." Pick a verse or use this one and begin this discipline with your daughter.

For "middle" girls—This stage of life is incredibly hard for girls. Their bodies are changing, and they are beginning to yearn for more independence. But they also can be very unsure of themselves. This is a great time for you to encourage your daughter to memorize a verse to remind her of her true identity in Christ. Look back over the verses we prayed in chapter 2 and pick one to memorize with your girl.

For big girls—Your daughter, like mine, is likely facing more situations where the results of her choices carry more significant consequences. Share with her how important it is to guard our minds with truth. James 1:5 is a great verse to memorize with your daughter, as it reminds us that God will give us wisdom if we ask.

13

Peaceful

May she allow God to grant her
deep peace in her mind.

And the peace of God, which surpasses all understanding, will
guard your hearts and your minds in Christ Jesus.

Philippians 4:7

Mommy, I so 'fraid," she said, lip trembling and tears about to fall.

Yes, I could have reminded her there was nothing to fear because she was safe in her bed in our home. But, to be honest, we'd had that conversation for the past several nights, and it wasn't proving effective at keeping her from waking me around 2:30 A.M. with that creepy awareness of someone staring at you while you sleep.

I resolved to try something new. I pulled out her Bible and showed her Psalm 56:3: "When I am afraid, I put my trust in you." I read it aloud and asked her to repeat it after me. We prayed for her to know that she was safe and that God is with her always. We asked Him to help her remember to put her trust in Him.

We had that same conversation several times over the next months. Eventually, Casiday's fear abated, and she began to sleep through the night.

Scripture has the power to bring peace to the chaos and fear in our minds. I think we often forget that—for ourselves and for our girls. I love Paul's words to the church at Philippi:

> Do not be anxious about anything, but in everything by prayer and supplication with thanksgiving let your requests be made known to God. And the peace of God, which surpasses all understanding, will guard your hearts and your minds in Christ Jesus.

> Philippians 4:6–7

Lately I've been studying Philippians. This morning I spent some time in these two verses. A large part of how I study the Bible involves writing out the verses I'm studying and underlining and capitalizing words that stand out to me. Here is what these verses looked like in my journal:

DO NOT be anxious about ANYTHING, but in EVERYTHING by prayer and supplication <u>with thanksgiving</u> let your requests <u>be made known</u> TO GOD. And <u>the peace of God</u>, which SURPASSES ALL UNDERSTANDING, will guard <u>your hearts and your minds</u> IN CHRIST JESUS.

I suppose because I'm a Bible teacher at heart, it only makes sense that I note what I've found in those verses about having a peaceful mind.

Understanding Peace

First, we must understand what peace is. The peace of God isn't the absence of conflict or difficulty. Rather, it is the assurance of His sovereignty, presence, and care that transcends our circumstances. Once we understand what peace is, we begin to understand this peace *of* God can only come *from* God. Isaiah 26:3 explains, "You keep him in perfect peace whose mind is stayed on you, because he trusts in you."

This is a peace we can't manufacture on our own. God keeps us at peace when we keep our mind stayed on Him. (For more on having a mind stayed on Christ, see chapter 10.) If we want to experience true peace, we must be fully aware we cannot do anything to create or sustain it. We must continually lay our thoughts and concerns down before the Lord. In Philippians 4:6, Paul makes this clear when he tells his readers to make their requests known to God.

Far too often we take our requests to everyone but God. We vent to our friends or share with our Bible study group. But the key to experiencing the peace of God is understanding that it can only come from God. This is an important truth we need to teach our girls. When they face the difficult seasons and deal with hard relationships, we must remind them that the peace they seek won't come from having friends who affirm them, but rather from the God who accepts them.

Undermining Peace

Once we understand what peace is and where we get it, we must consider the ways we can undermine the process of experiencing it. Again, we look at Paul's words and see his strong admonition at the beginning: "Do not be anxious about anything. . . ."

Jesus addressed this topic as well: "Peace I leave with you; my peace I give to you. Not as the world gives do I give to you. Let not your hearts be troubled, neither let them be afraid" (John 14:27). Jesus talked about our hearts being troubled and afraid. So often, the feelings of our heart result in the worries of our mind.

Most of us can remember wondering why someone didn't want to play with us on the playground or the anxiety we felt in middle school about our appearance or abilities. These feelings can be magnified for our girls as they get older and are more engaged on social media. The real-time awareness of being left out or the sense of not being enough is hard to avoid when friends are posting photos of their activities while our girls are sitting at home wondering why no one included them.

Our daughters need us to point them back to truth when those feelings of insecurity and uncertainty begin to undermine the peace Christ offers. They need us to remind them of God's sovereignty and love. I often turn to verses like this one: "And he is before all things, and in him all things hold together," to help remind Casiday of God's never-ceasing awareness and control of all things (Colossians 1:17).

When it feels like the world is spinning out of control and peace seems impossible to find, the simple reminder that it is Christ holding all things together can bring comfort to an anxious heart.

Unfathomable Peace

My favorite phrase in Philippians 4:7 is "which surpasses all understanding." Isn't that a wonderful thought? We can't possibly understand the peace He gives; it doesn't make sense. It just is.

Paul told the Colossians to let this peace of Christ "rule" in their hearts (Colossians 3:15). The Prince of peace is the One who holds it all together. We can trust Him, and we can find refuge in this promise.

Don't miss this! The refuge and rest we find in Christ is not rooted in our feelings, but rather in His person. He is peace. Period. And when we set our minds on Him, when we allow His Word to renew and guard our minds, we will know a peace that makes no sense to those around us, a peace we cannot fully explain but can only experience.

Casiday's fears about monsters lurking in her room seem silly to her now. But that verse we said together every night when she was four came back around when she was thirteen. In the middle of those ever-challenging tween years, a new set of fears found their way into her heart. One night we were again in her room, both of us lying in her bed, rehashing some of the rough stuff she faced that week at school.

She said, "Mom, is it always going to be like this? Am I always going to be afraid of something or someone?" I told her I hoped not, and reminded her God has not given her that spirit of fear, but one of boldness and confidence (2 Timothy 1:7).

We lay there quietly for a few minutes, and then she said, "You know what verse I really love right now? Psalm 56:3."

I chuckled and asked her if she remembered the first time she'd heard that verse. She didn't, so I told her the story. Then together we said, "When I am afraid, I will put my trust in you."

PRAYERS

Lord, I pray _____ will set her mind on the hope she has in You. May her mind be focused, guarded by the grace You have given her. (1 Peter 1:13)

Lord, Your Word is the sword that protects us. May _____
_____ realize it is living and active, and that it is able
to help her discern truth and find peace through Christ.
(Hebrews 4:12)

Lord, there will be seasons when _____ feels her
faith slipping away. She'll long for the peace she's known
in You. When those days come, I pray she will remember
what she knows, what she's learned. May her mind recall
Your Word, even when her feelings don't. (Philippians 3:16)

Lord, _____ will undoubtedly experience
times of discord with others. When those days come, may
she allow the peace she has in You to guide her in living
at peace with others. May her mind lead her toward encouragement and unity. (Romans 14:19)

Lord, when situations arise and _____ has to
make a choice, I pray she will remember Your Word, will
remember Whose she is, and will choose to pursue what
is right and good in Your sight. (Psalm 34:14)

Lord, I pray _____ will remember that she
can cast all her fears and cares and worries on You. May
she rest in the truth that You care for her, You value her,
and You love her. (1 Peter 5:7)

Lord, it's Your peace that guards our hearts and minds.
May _____ know this truth and rest in it. I pray
she will be surrounded by the indescribable peace You
offer. (Philippians 4:7)

Lord, may _____ learn to take every thought
captive. May she train her mind to seek Your heart, and

may she be deliberate in choosing to obey You. (2 Corinthians 10:5)

Lord, I pray _____ keeps her gaze straight in front of her. May she not be distracted by the things on the left and on the right. May her focus be on You. (Proverbs 4:25)

Lord, the things of this world are sparkly and shiny. They look good on the surface, but they won't last. I pray _____ will not be enticed by the worthless treasures on earth, but will instead seek the eternal things of heaven. (Psalm 119:37)

Just for Moms

What are you afraid of? What keeps you from experiencing the true peace of God in your life?

I'll make it easy and go first: I worry that Casiday won't ever deeply love the Lord, that she'll become a master at playing the church game and miss out on the rich love He has for her. I also worry she's going to make bad decisions as a teenager that will impact the rest of her life. I play out every worst-case scenario. And fear gets a stronghold in my mind.

Maybe you know what I mean? How do we battle that? We remember that we're not called to fear but to faith. (And yes, that's totally a Sunday school–type answer.) Here is what I do when I find fear is gaining a stronghold in my thoughts: I make a list of all the things I'm afraid of. I write them out, no matter how crazy or unlikely they are. And then I write over them what God's Word says. I cover my fears and anxieties with the truth of His Word. Even when I don't feel it, I choose to believe it.

Next time you're overwhelmed by anxieties and fears, I urge you to try the same thing.

Lord, we mommas are top-notch worriers. In fact, if it were an Olympic sport, we could be gold medalists. But You have called us to something far better than fear and worry. You invite us to walk in faith and peace. And, God, that is truly what we long for. We want the unfathomable peace only You can give. Help us to quit settling for a temporary peace we can manufacture. Give us an urgency for the deep peace You offer, the truest peace that transcends our situations, circumstances, and emotions. Give us the courage to trust You with our babies, knowing You love them even more than we do, and Your plans for them are good and trustworthy. Grant us the peace that passes all understanding and let us walk in faith. In Jesus' name, Amen.

Girl Talk

For little girls—Ask your daughter what scares her. Tell her about something that scares you. Let her write out her fear or draw a picture of something that scares her. Then share with her that God is bigger than anything we're afraid of, and we can always trust Him to protect us and give us peace. Look up Psalm 56:3 and read it to your daughter. Let her write the verse over her picture or words. Remind her that our faith covers our fears.

For "middle" girls—Plan a mother-daughter outing to someplace you find peaceful. Talk with your daughter about what you like about being there. Ask her what makes her feel peaceful. Read Isaiah 26:3 with her. Talk about some situations where it's hard to feel peaceful and remind her that even in those times she can know the peace God gives.

For big girls—As our girls start making decisions about what classes to take in high school, what colleges to apply to, and what their college major will be, it can be overwhelming (for them and for us). This is a great time to plan a whole day (or maybe even an overnight trip) to spend with your girl. Make it a point to include some downtime in the schedule. While you are together, ask her what she's worried about or afraid of concerning her future. Just listen to her and let her share at her own pace. You'll want to give the easy answers, but don't! When you get home, take some time to write down her concerns. Write her a note sharing what you loved about your time together and assure her you are praying over the things she told you. Share Philippians 4:6–7 or another verse that has been helpful to you when you worry.

PART 4

Prayers for Her Relationships

Often, when we talk about relationships, we focus on the specific types of relationships, like parent-child and husband-wife. This section, however, explores characteristics our girls need to be successful in any relationship. While there are countless qualities that nurture positive relational experiences, these chapters focus on four we see vividly in Christ: humility, wisdom, generosity, and love.

14

Humility

May she exhibit the humility of
Christ in all her relationships.

Put on then, as God's chosen ones, holy and beloved, compassionate hearts, kindness, humility, meekness, and patience.

Colossians 3:12

Dress-up was a huge part of our daughter's childhood.
My mom sewed her countless costumes, including ball
gowns, gypsy dresses, and even a wedding dress complete
with long veil. Scott's grandmother was the favorite to an-
nounce Casiday's fashion shows, as she always had a way
of describing each outfit as if it were truly from a high-end
couture line in Paris.

With a sixteen-year-old, dress-up looks a little different.
Mostly I find myself being asked, "Mom, what do you think
about this for school tomorrow?" or maybe, "Does this look

okay for church?" There is the occasional, "Can I borrow this?" as she walks through the house wearing one of my scarves, sweaters, or necklaces. (My shoes are too small, so they remain safe in my closet. Small gifts, people, small gifts.)

I used to wonder if, when I encouraged Casiday's interest in dress-up and figuring out what to wear, I was also teaching her the wrong lessons. But these verses caught my eye a few years ago:

> Put on then, as God's chosen ones, holy and beloved, compassionate hearts, kindness, humility, meekness, and patience, bearing with one another and, if one has a complaint against another, forgiving each other; as the Lord has forgiven you, so you also must forgive. And above all these put on love, which binds everything together in perfect harmony.
>
> Colossians 3:12–14

What to Wear

Put on. Paul is instructing the church at Colossae (and all of us) about what we should be wearing as believers. In fact, in the New International Version, Colossians 3:12 specifically says "clothe yourselves." I'm certainly not suggesting that the issue of skinny jeans and fringe boots is equal in significance to God's desire for us to be clothed in compassion and kindness. But Scripture gives us a great deal of description about what we are to "wear" as believers, much the same as Mamaw provided plenty of details about Casiday's dress-up ensembles.

When we look at what characteristics should be evident in a believer's life—attributes that should define the way we conduct ourselves among others, traits that should manifest themselves in all our relationships—we might all make slightly different lists. It wasn't easy to narrow down this part of the book to just four characteristics. My goal was to identify four overarching qualities that would encompass the innumerable facets of being a godly friend, spouse, parent, or employee.

Over the next four chapters, we'll be exploring four ways we can pray for our girls to clothe themselves—four manners of thinking and acting that will profoundly affect every relationship in their lives. We'll start with one the world most often reviles: humility.

A Humble Spirit

Our best example of humility is, of course, Christ. Paul provides a beautiful portrait of this in Philippians 2:5–8:

> Have this mind among yourselves, which is yours in Christ Jesus, who, though he was in the form of God, did not count equality with God a thing to be grasped, but emptied himself, by taking the form of a servant, being born in the likeness of men. And being found in human form, he humbled himself by becoming obedient to the point of death, even death on a cross.

Humility of spirit is revealed in two ways: emptying ourselves and embracing obedience. In the margin of my Bible, I have this note written to myself about verse 7, "What needs emptying in me?" What are the things I cling to, the abilities or accomplishments I stake as the center of my identity? Jesus, though He was fully God, emptied himself of all the accoutrements of heaven, all the glory He was due, choosing to be identified as a slave, a bondservant. Compared with that, what do I have worth holding on to?

It's important for us to remind our girls that all those things they chase, like popularity, achievement, and success, fade in comparison to having the humble spirit of Christ.

A Humble Servant

Christ's humble spirit enabled Him to be a humble servant to others. John 13:1–20 is perhaps the most poignant illustration of Jesus' love for and service to His disciples. Take a moment to read this passage.

One of the most moving worship services I've ever been a part of was several years ago when we were still in Georgia. Our pastor called a few people to come up to the platform at our church. As they each sat down in the chairs that were set up, he walked behind them, talking about the ways each one had served in our church and in our community. Then he slowly knelt before each one, washing their feet and telling them how their service had impacted his life.

Not one person in the church left with dry eyes that morning, because true, humble service impacts everyone who sees it. As our pastor spoke about each of those people, many of us could have shared our own stories of how they had ministered to us or how their testimonies had impacted our lives.

But the truth is, the four or five people sitting in those chairs were probably the most uncomfortable people in the building. Not one of them had ever done anything for the sake of recognition. Each of them would gladly have stepped aside, out of the limelight, in order to celebrate and honor someone else. Oh, that we would raise daughters like this!

True Beauty

Peter was one of those men who had his feet washed by Jesus. Just a few verses later in John 13, Jesus told Peter he would deny Him three times that night. Peter's third denial was accompanied by the crowing of a rooster. Peter's pride is evident throughout the Gospels and even in some portions of Acts. And yet, by the time he wrote his epistles, we see the heart of a man who had learned the hard lessons of humility.

That's why his words in 1 Peter 3, below, are so powerful to me, because he had battled the desire for recognition and reward. When he wrote to husbands and wives about how to interact with one another, it wasn't from a heart of judgment or condemnation. By this point Peter had been married for a while and had, no doubt, learned some valuable lessons about the nature of relationships between men and women. (Remember, Jesus had healed Peter's mother-in-law, as recorded in Matthew 8:14–15.)

I'll be honest, Peter's words in 1 Peter 3:3–4 have always been a bit of a challenge to an outspoken, high-energy girl like me:

> Do not let your adorning be external—the braiding of hair and the putting on of gold jewelry, or the clothing you wear—but let your adorning be the hidden person of the heart with the imperishable beauty of a gentle and quiet spirit, which in God's sight is very precious.

Not once in my whole life has anyone ever used the phrase "quiet and gentle" to describe me. But the heart behind these words is what we all need to pursue. God says this manner of spirit is of imperishable beauty. It won't fade or go out of style. How do we convey this to our girls? How can we help them understand that God's concern isn't what they wear or how they do their hair, but rather about the character of their hearts. Are we raising daughters who are humble and gentle?

In a world that tells our girls their beauty is all about what is seen by people, may we be the moms who remind them (and ourselves) that the true beauty God desires is reflected not by mastering the perfect smoky eye, but by learning to see others the way He does. And as we see them, to serve and care for them as He has served and cared for us.

PRAYERS

Lord, while so many women in our culture spend their energy and resources on outward beauty, I pray _____ will know it is her inner loveliness that pleases You. May she nourish her spirit, pursuing a gentleness that speaks of Your work in her life. (1 Peter 3:3–4)

Lord, I pray my girl will allow herself to be humbled by You. May _____ realize that the honor You offer to those who are humble is far greater than anything the world can give to those who are prideful. (1 Peter 5:6)

Lord, may _____ grow in gentleness and patience and humility. I pray her life will be a testimony to Your work in her heart. May she always be faithful to deal with others in love, the way You have dealt with her. (Ephesians 4:2)

Lord, just as John the Baptist prayed, "He must increase, but I must decrease," may _____ have that same desire. May she long to see Your name known, and may her desire be to point others toward You and not toward herself. (John 3:30)

Lord, thank You for making clear what You desire for us, especially in our dealings with others. I pray _____ will be faithful to Your Word. May she live justly, love mercy, and walk humbly with You for her whole life. (Micah 6:8)

Lord, in a world where competition, comparison, and conniving seem to rule the day, I pray _____ will have a humble heart. May she always "count others more significant" and be willing to lay aside her preferences and desires, following the example of Christ in all her dealings with others. (Philippians 2:3)

Lord, there are days when I see that pride and haughtiness well up in my girl. May _____ be quick to recognize that in herself and to confess it to You. May she choose instead to live in harmony with others, never ignoring or demeaning anyone. (Romans 12:16)

Lord, may the freedom _____ has in You motivate her to serve others. May she never take advantage of anyone. Give her a humble heart that seeks the best for others in every situation, always pointing them toward You. (Galatians 5:13)

Lord, I pray _____ will have a deep desire to live at peace with others. May she be quick to give the benefit of the doubt and be willing to humble herself for the purpose of unity within the Body. (Hebrews 12:14)

Lord, You tell us that when we humble ourselves before You, we can trust that You will lift us up. I pray _____ will lean into this truth and walk with humility. (James 4:10)

Just for Moms

Can I tell you something I wish weren't true about myself? Sometimes I get resentful of how much time I spend serving my family. I love them, and my people are really good at saying thank you and helping out when things are crazy. But some days it feels like all I do is pick up after people and do things for other people, and I just want to tell them, "I'm done! You all have to serve me today!"

But every time I get to that point, the Lord reminds me of the way He serves me. And I think about the ever-present dishes in the sink and all the times I move the backpack into Casiday's bedroom from the chair in the living room where she leaves it, and I realize these really aren't a big deal. When I'm folding the thousandth load of laundry, I can choose to be resentful of the excess or thankful for the abundance. Maybe you need to make that choice too sometimes? You're not alone. But God has a better desire for us than the bitterness and resentment that come from our pride. He's not just calling our daughters to humility and service in their relationships. He is calling us to the same.

Lord, sometimes we feel unappreciated and even unseen. We love our families and our churches, and we want to serve others. We long for humble spirits like Yours. Will You help us to see the ways our actions and our attitudes can influence our families? Give us humble hearts and a willingness to serve, not for our sake, but for Yours. Grant us wisdom to teach our girls the beauty of a gentle and quiet spirit isn't about personality, but about humility. Open our eyes to the ways we can serve, and help us do it with humble and gracious hearts. In Jesus' name, Amen.

Girl Talk

For little girls—Let your daughter help you sort or fold laundry. As you work together, remind her she is serving the whole family. Talk with her about the ways Jesus served others and His desire for us to be willing to serve as well.

For "middle" girls—Do your daughter's least-favorite chore for her. When she realizes you have already done it, talk with her about the ways serving others has been an encouragement for you. Help her identify ways she can serve in your family or church. Remind her how important it is for us to serve humbly, without needing recognition or reward. Read Philippians 2:3 with her and remind her that God is looking at our hearts when we serve.

For big girls—Read 1 Peter 3:3–4 with your daughter. Talk with her about how easy it is to focus on our outside when what really matters is what is inside us. Discuss how having a "quiet and gentle spirit" impacts our relationships with others, and help her identify ways she can reflect the humble spirit of Christ in her life.

15

Wisdom

May she have wisdom in all her relationships.

Who is wise and understanding among you? By his good conduct let him show his works in the meekness of wisdom.

James 3:13

Sometimes I have the opportunity to share simple Bible lessons with the children in our church. One thing I know is the lesson can't last too long because these kids are ready for the snack. On one occasion, I asked if any of them had ever said something they wish they hadn't. Hands shot up, children anxious to share their stories of misspoken words. As I told them about the power of our words, I squeezed toothpaste onto a small paper plate. I knew their attention was on my actions more than my words.

As the tube emptied, I asked one of the girls if she could get all the toothpaste on the plate back into the tube. She laughed and said it's impossible. I smiled and affirmed her answer.

Then I reminded them it's also impossible for us to take back our words.

It's a simple lesson, but the power of that illustration haunts me. How do we learn to use our words, our lives, in a manner that leaves it all out there, messy and in plain view, but with no desire to push it back into the hidden places, where no one can judge our inadequacies and see our insecurities?

Wisdom.

It's the answer to so many questions we ask as believers. Like Solomon, we realize our need for this insight and understanding that can come only from the Lord. It's the necessary ingredient to navigating the ever-more-foolish world in which we live.

As moms, we know all about praying for wisdom, right? Rarely does a day pass when I don't utter a prayer rooted in the words of James: "If any of you lacks wisdom, let him ask God, who gives generously to all without reproach, and it will be given him" (James 1:5).

Lord, give me wisdom to find a plan to help this baby sleep.

Lord, give me wisdom to know what to do about these tantrums.

Lord, give me wisdom about how to educate my child.

Lord, give me wisdom to guide her through these tween years.

Lord, give me wisdom as we prepare her to live on her own, outside the safety of our home.

And the prayers for wisdom never cease. As long as we're mommas, we'll be praying for wisdom to teach and guide and mentor our girls. As well we should.

But what about praying for our girls to have wisdom? Are we as diligent about that? Sometimes I think it's easier for us to pray for wisdom to tell them what to do rather than praying for them to have wisdom to make the choices for themselves.

As we explore how and why we need to pray for our girls to have wisdom in their relationships, we'll be looking at three specific areas, discussed throughout Scripture, as we develop a framework for prayers that our daughters will walk in wisdom.

Wisdom in Conversations

> Set a guard, O Lord, over my mouth; keep watch over the door of my lips!
>
> Psalm 141:3

Let's be honest here, more often than not, it's less the words our girls say and more the tone with which they say them that lands them in trouble. If I had a nickel for every time I've told Casiday, "It's HOW you said it!" well, let's just say we could definitely take that dream trip to Italy.

Helping our girls understand the significance of both the verbal and nonverbal aspects of communication is vital. And with social media, it's even harder! I know my child has sent a text or a tweet that she would never even consider speaking out loud.

Moms, we have to step up! Our girls need us to watch their words—spoken and written (and even to some extent the emojis they use). Helping our girls learn to navigate conversations with grace and wisdom is one of our most important jobs.

When Casiday was little, Scott's family sometimes got frustrated with me because they felt I was too hard on her about how she spoke and carried herself. I can remember saying, "You hate it now, I know. But in ten years, when she's a polite and kind teenager, you'll be glad." And it's true. For the most part, I don't worry too much about how Casiday speaks or acts around adults. We regularly hear from others how well-mannered she is and what a joy it is to be around her.

But that doesn't mean I can rest on my laurels. I am still very much in the training season, especially as it relates to her relationships with others. Helping her understand the power of her words is a key part of guiding her toward wisdom.

Wisdom in Circumstances

So flee youthful passions and pursue righteousness, faith, love, and peace, along with those who call on the Lord from a pure heart.

2 Timothy 2:22

All you moms with babies, I know it seems like what I'm about to cover is far, far away for you. But the truth is, we need to be teaching our girls from the time they are young how to navigate life with wisdom. We should have open, honest, and even awkward conversations with them about inappropriate places to be, things to watch, and activities to do.

We must give them the tools they need to get out of situations when they feel uncomfortable, and make sure they understand we are there to help them, even when they find themselves in over their heads. And—this one is so important—we need to show them that even when they make unwise choices, we will love them and, like the father of the prodigal son, we will watch for them and run to greet them, giving grace and welcoming them home (Luke 15:20).

In no way am I suggesting we should not discipline or allow natural consequences for our daughters' poor choices. Rather, that even in those times, we can be a voice of grace and kindness, which will hopefully lead them to repentance (Romans 2:4).

Wisdom in Companions

Whoever walks with the wise becomes wise, but the companion of fools will suffer harm.

Proverbs 13:20

Over the years, my daughter has had some friends who are, as my grandmother would say, humdingers. But she's also been fortunate to have some of the sweetest friendships that have survived our move from Georgia to Alabama. Right now, some of her closest friends are her cousins in Texas.

It doesn't take long to see how the companions our girls choose affect them, does it? We've been known to limit the time she spends with some friends because of the detoxing we end up doing when she gets back home. And there are girls she can be with who bring out the very best in her. Those are the ones we tend to like best.

Our girls are learning now how to be wise as they choose companions, from best friends on the playground to first boyfriends and even college roommates. As they get older, we have to learn when we should speak up and when we should let them learn the hard lessons (and sometimes, we find out the people we were sure were going to be horrible end up being the dearest friends our girls could have).

We must pray for wisdom about those we allow our girls to spend time with, but even more important, we should pray for them to have wisdom and discernment for themselves.

At the end of Casiday's sophomore year, after three years of cheerleading (two of them as the captain of her squad), she made the difficult decision not to try out for her junior year. She cried, I cried. We both second- and third-guessed her decision and mourned her loss of doing something she loved so much.

Her resolve to step away from the situation was rooted in her understanding of how the dynamics of the girls on the squad were affecting her. I knew it was the right choice. All those prayers for her to have wisdom, to be discerning, and even to have courage to stand up for herself were coming true.

While the first two years of high school were full of tears, self-loathing, anxiety, and doubt, her junior year has been filled with new friends, greater confidence, and a sense of purpose I wasn't sure we'd ever see.

Moms, those prayers you're praying matter! It may take a lot of heartache, a lot of tears, and a few hard decisions, but you'll see the work of God in your girl; you'll see her display the wisdom you prayed she'd have. And, on this side of it all, I can promise you it's worth it!

PRAYERS

Lord, may _____ walk in wisdom in all her relationships, but especially with those people who don't know You. May her demeanor be gracious and her words wise as she seeks opportunities to share Your love with others. (Colossians 4:5–6)

Lord, I pray _____ will be wise, living in a manner that pleases You. May she manage her time well so she can build relationships with others. Help her learn to see the value of time spent with people and be willing to invest in relationships. (Ephesians 5:15–16)

Lord, _____ will have difficult relationships. There will be times when she doesn't know what to do. I pray that when those days come, she will remember to come to You for wisdom. May she have confidence that You will hear her request and answer her generously. (James 1:5)

Lord, wisdom is so much more than knowledge. I pray my girl will long for Your wisdom and pursue it with fervor. And as _____ grows in wisdom, may her dealings with others reflect You and the kindness with which You deal with us. (James 3:13)

Lord, we all need wisdom. Help _____ recognize that all wisdom comes from You. May she seek Your guidance as she navigates relationships with others, trusting Your leading to help her treat others well. (Proverbs 2:6)

Lord, I pray _____ will realize it is the wisdom she gains from You that will help her live her life well. May she lean into Your Word as her guide and trust Your Spirit to lead her always. As she prepares for every day, may seeking You be a priority. (Psalm 90:12)

Lord, so often our words reveal our lack of wisdom and self-control. I pray _____ will learn early the value of guarding her speech, the wisdom of saying less. May she use her words to encourage and build up those around her. (Proverbs 13:3)

Lord, may _____ seek You above all. Of all the choices she will ever make, the wisest one is following You. And as she follows You, I pray she will grow in every way and live a life that draws others to You. (Ephesians 1:17)

Lord, may _____ be wise in choosing her companions. I pray she will seek out relationships with those who are faithful to You and Your Word. May she surround herself with friends who will encourage her in her faith. (Psalm 119:63)

Lord, I pray _____ turns from evil and chooses good. May she seek Your peace and pursue a life that pleases You. (1 Peter 3:11)

Just for Moms

When our girls make unwise choices, it's hard not to intervene. But there are times when we can push in and inadvertently disrupt the work God is doing in their lives. (Trust me on this one. I've got the T-shirt to prove I was there.)

If your daughter is walking that line between wise and unwise—pray, pray, pray! Speak truth over her and into her. But also, especially as she gets older, trust the Lord to speak into her heart in a way you can't. It's the hardest thing we will do. I know.

Sometimes they don't listen. Sometimes, they will rush headlong into the most destructive places, and we will wish we had done more, wish we had said more. Even then, sweet mom, can I just remind you that these girls of ours make their own choices? We can't control their every move. And no matter what they do, no matter how far they go, and as much as we want them to come home, God longs even more for them to return to Him.

Lord, there are days when all we can do is wonder how we failed so badly. How we could have raised a girl who would make such profoundly unwise choices. And sometimes in our despair, we may even wonder how You could still love us in light of the complete mess readily apparent in our families. When those days come, will You wrap us up in Your comfort? Remind us there is nothing we or our daughters can do to separate ourselves from Your love. When we cry, help us remember that You are capturing every tear in a bottle, and that Your heart aches for our girls and for us because we are all Your girls. Speak peace into our wounded hearts, grace into our weary souls, and truth into our worrying minds. Give us strength to trust in You, especially on the hardest days. In Jesus' name, Amen.

Girl Talk

For little girls—Do a little role-playing with your daughter, acting out situations where you are a good friend and where you are a bad friend. Talk with her about how she can respond when someone is unkind or wants her to do something she knows she shouldn't.

For "middle" girls—Set aside some time to talk with your girl about what makes a good friend. Ask her to make a list of what qualities she thinks good friends have. Look over the list with her and discuss how she can work to develop those traits in her own life.

For big girls—BFFs, frenemies, mean girls . . . at this age, relationships between girls can be just terrifying. And when you toss boyfriends or crushes into the mix, it moves from terrifying to borderline insanity, right? Now is when she needs you more than ever to be the voice of reason. She may not like what you say, she may not even like you. But have the hard conversations about what you observe in her relationships, what you expect of her, and most of all, what God expects. And even on the hardest days, remind her you love her and believe in the future God has for her.

Generosity

May her life be marked
by a generous spirit in every way.

For they all contributed out of their abundance, but she out of
her poverty put in all she had.

Luke 21:4

This is for you. Don't open it now, just know how much you mean to me." My friend slid an envelope into my hands, hugged me tight, and then climbed into her car and drove away. When I peeked in the envelope, tears began flowing down my cheeks. One thousand dollars.

One. Thousand. Dollars.

Y'all, I don't know about you, but that sort of thing does not happen in my world. At least, it never had until that moment. For the Underwoods, it was huge. HUGE.

About twenty years before the thousand-dollar incident, I'd experienced another sort of generosity.

I was basically a disaster from the ages of nineteen to twenty-two. I mean, if there was a bad choice to make, I made it, and usually in the most dramatic manner possible. My specific choices and consequences really aren't the issue, though. The point is where I finally hit rock bottom.

One Friday night in January of 1995, I sat in my bedroom in Huntsville, Alabama, and began swallowing a bottle of Valium, one pill every ten minutes until I passed out. I woke up in the hospital looking at my dad, who had driven through the night to be there with me. I was broken, a mess of emotions, regret, and grief. And yet, there he was, this man who had always loved me, always believed in me, and always spoken truth to me.

I moved back to Missouri to live with my parents. I saw a Christian counselor, got involved in church, and joined a Bible study group. And slowly I found myself at peace with God and, even more significantly, desperate to give my life over to serving Him.

That little church in northeast Missouri was the place God began to show me the grace and mercy He has for all of us. Those people loved me and prayed for me, and encouraged me as I did the hard work of admitting the sin in my life and grieving for the sorrow my choices had brought to people I love.

The Many Forms of Generosity

Often when I think of someone being generous, the image of my friend's financial gift comes to mind. And, yes, that is a beautiful example of heartfelt generosity. But generosity can take many forms, and we must help our girls learn to see how a generous spirit can impact her relationships and even those outside her circle of influence.

One of my favorite biblical accounts of generosity is found in Luke 21:1–4. Take a moment to read this familiar story of the widow and her offering.

So good, right? I love what Jesus says: "But she out of her poverty put in all she had to live on" (Luke 21:4). True generosity can only come from a recognition of our deep poverty. It happens when we realize that nothing we have is really ours anyway.

I often tell the story of Scott's and my first date. It was sort of an awkward thing, but we ended up at Hardee's eating hamburgers together before he left my small Missouri town to return to his home in Alabama. After we'd ordered and were sitting in the booth ready to eat, Scott prayed over our food, and I will never forget what he said: "Lord, thank You for this food and thank You for the money You provided to purchase it."

I knew right then that there was something different about this singer from Alabama, and I was really sure I wanted to get to know him better. (Less than a year later we were married, so that worked out pretty well.)

Generosity is less about what we give and more about the heart behind our giving.

Generous Encouragement

Do you know people who are quick to encourage? My love language is words of affirmation, so I'm always drawn to people who are great encouragers. My mother-in-law is this kind of person. She is quick to compliment, but it's more than that. She is a true encourager. And she is generous in doing so. It is a quality I have observed in her for over twenty years, and one I want to grow in my own life.

Do you encourage your daughter to be an encourager of others? One year in middle school Casiday tried out for a solo in show choir. She didn't get it, but I'll never forget what she said. "It's okay, Mom. Susan really did a great job. She is perfect for that song." And when she chose not to try out for cheerleading, she sent texts to the girls who were trying out to tell them good luck and that she was praying for them.

Nurture these instincts in your girls if they have them. And if your girl isn't a natural encourager, pray for her to become one.

Generous Equipping

Two of my dearest friends are women I have met through blogging. Both are quick to share what they have learned with me and have helped me become a better blogger and writer. In a world where far too many women look at everyone else as competition, it's a gift to have women like these two who are on "my team" and who share their knowledge and their experiences to help me reach my goals.

What if we raised daughters who had that same mentality? Girls who didn't just cheer each other on, but shared the best of what they knew and could do to help others achieve their dreams and reach their goals. Paul told the Philippians to look out for the interests of others (Philippians 2:4). When we seek out the best for others, we find ourselves willing to sacrifice and share what we have and know for their benefit. Let's be moms who pray for our girls to have this kind of heart.

Generous Estate

I can't really write about generosity without touching on our financial and material resources. Are we raising girls who see us being generous, even sacrificial, with our money? Or do they see us spending money to keep up appearances?

The little woman in the temple who gave all she had is a powerful challenge to me. I've often thought I don't know much about true sacrifice. I've never had to choose between giving a meal to someone else and providing food for my daughter. I've never been in a position of giving up something I need so someone else can have something they need even more.

And the truth is, our girls probably haven't either. But we need to teach them to be generous. To realize, as Scott prayed, that the money we have for our food, our clothes, our activities, our homes, our cars, for everything we have, it all comes from God. And even the jobs we have are the result of His gracious provision in our lives.

If we're serious about raising girls who seek the Lord, there is no escaping the expectation for generosity to be a prevailing characteristic in their lives. And we need to remember the same is true for us as well.

PRAYERS

Lord, in a world that constantly says to get what you can for yourself, I pray _____ will have a heart that seeks the best for others. May she look for ways to help and serve others, even when it may not appear to be what is best for herself. (1 Corinthians 10:24)

Lord, may _____ be generous with herself, not just her possessions. I pray she will have a tenderness with others, a gentleness that points to You. May she be sympathetic to others, always acting in abounding love. (1 Peter 3:8)

Lord, it's so easy for us to want all the praise and recognition we can garner. I pray, though, that my girl will

be generous with her encouragement of others. May
_____ use her words and abilities to build
up others, as You are faithful to build her up. (1 Thessalonians 5:11)

Lord, I pray _____ will be a cheerful giver.
May she never grow so attached to her resources that she
fails to see opportunities to be generous and meet the
needs of others. (2 Corinthians 9:7)

Lord, just as You have graciously and generously borne
our burdens, may _____ be willing to
come alongside others and help them carry their loads.
May she have a compassionate heart that seeks to support
and encourage others. (Galatians 6:2)

Lord, may _____ never fail to see the injustice around her. May she be bold in speaking against
oppression, and may she defend those who cannot defend
themselves. I pray she will be generous in helping others,
especially the helpless. (Isaiah 1:17)

Lord, in an incredibly skeptical world, I pray my girl will be
incredibly generous. Give _____ a heart
that values people over possessions and a mind that understands sacrificial living is a beautiful way to worship
You. (Luke 6:30)

Lord, I pray _____ will use her resources, her
words, and her abilities to reach out to others. May she
find great joy in giving and serving those in need around
her. (Proverbs 11:25)

Lord, we live in a world that loves to bend the rules and find the loopholes. I pray _____ will live with integrity, conducting her life with honor and justice, and dealing generously with everyone she meets. (Psalm 112:5)

Lord, may _____ be quick to turn the other cheek, not seeking revenge or retribution. Instead, may she have a heart that seeks to do good, to encourage and reach out to others. (1 Thessalonians 5:15)

Just for Moms

One of my favorite books on the topic of generosity is Kristen Welch's *Raising Grateful Kids in an Entitled World*. Kristen's life was radically changed when she went on a trip with Compassion International several years ago. Since then, her family has begun a nonprofit, and she is actively involved in helping women around the world learn trades to provide them with sustainable income.

Kristen's whole family has been turned upside down by what God is doing in them. She regularly writes on her blog about how it isn't always easy and the ways she and the other members of her family struggle with this life God has called them to live.[1]

My situation isn't like Kristen's. Yours may not be either. And that's okay. But we do know the restlessness and tension between living the way Scripture leads and wanting to fit into the world around us. He's called me to be me. And He's called you to be you. It's not a competition for who can give more or better. The question for all of us is the same: "How is God calling me to live generously and sacrificially in my world right now?"

Lord, I pray You'll give us hearts of generosity, willing to give sacrificially as You lead. Help us nurture that same desire in the hearts and lives of our girls. Open our eyes to the needs around us, and move us into action. When we start to compare ourselves to others, give us wisdom to stop and seek You alone. May we act in a manner that points to You always. And may we, like the woman in the temple, give all we have for Your sake. In Jesus' name, Amen.

Girl Talk

For little girls—If your little girl is anything like mine was, you probably have a few zoos' worth of stuffed animals in your home. Take some time to sort through all those critters with your daughter and invite her to select a few to donate to other children. If you want it to be a more personal experience, contact your local fire or police department. Many times they keep small stuffed animals in their vehicles to give to the children with whom they interact.

For "middle" girls—One of the greatest lessons we can teach our girls is to be generous with others. During this season of life, it's likely your daughter is dealing with some difficult friendships. Make some time to talk with her about giving the benefit of the doubt to her friends. Sometimes the generosity we most need is for someone to assume the best about us rather than the worst.

For big girls—At this age, time may be your daughter's most valuable commodity. But teaching her to give her time for others needs to be a priority. Brainstorm with her about ways she could sacrifice some time to encourage others. For example, she could offer free baby-sitting to a single mom or help tutor another student in her school.

17

Love

May she display a genuine love
for others throughout her life.

Beloved, let us love one another, for love is from God, and whoever loves has been born of God.

1 John 4:7

Have you ever felt left out? Unnoticed? Even unloved? I would guess at some point we all have. And because we know those feelings, we would do anything we could to make sure our girls never experience them.

More than once I've watched Casiday's face fall as she saw yet another picture on Instagram of a group of girls together when she wasn't included. Even when she might not have wanted to go, it still stings not even to be asked.

Sadly, we live in a world that is far quicker to say "Not you!" than it is to welcome with the words "You too!" Our girls can find themselves excluded for reasons like their appearance, their address, and even their willingness to accept others.

One of the most important traits we can pray for and nurture in our girls is that they are loving toward others. Jesus said it's our love for others that will reveal our commitment to Him (John 13:34–35). In Luke 19 we find the story of someone who had likely heard "Not you!" more times than he could count. Read the account of Jesus and Zacchaeus in Luke 19:1–10.

Zacchaeus seemed to have it made. Though his job as a tax collector may not have made him the most popular guy in Jericho, his financial status undoubtedly opened at least a few doors for him. Of course, if you know Zacchaeus's story, you know that what was visible didn't give the full picture.

We can learn some important lessons about what loving others looks like through Zacchaeus's story, lessons to teach our girls and to apply in our own lives.

Love looks beyond appearances. A gaping void pushed Zacchaeus up that sycamore tree to see the rabbi who healed and fed and welcomed. I always picture a stubby little man, full around the middle, clinging to the branches of that tree, desperate to find out if this Jesus everyone was talking about would be different from any of the other teachers who had wandered their way through Judea.

Jesus saw beyond what Zacchaeus looked like and what he did. Just as God had done when looking over Jesse's sons to find a new king for His people, Jesus looked at the heart of the man, not just his appearance (1 Samuel 16:7).

We are called to do the same thing.

Love extends acceptance. Zacchaeus wasn't just short of stature, he was short of acceptance. I think Zacchaeus might have felt like Jesus was his last chance. And Jesus, by inviting himself to Zacchaeus's home, gave this little man in the tree what he had been looking for—acceptance.

May we pray for and teach our daughters to see beyond appearances and extend acceptance to those who so desperately need to feel a sense of belonging.

Love offers approval. I love what Jesus says to Zacchaeus: "Today salvation has come to this house, since he also is a son of Abraham. For the Son of Man came to seek and to save the lost" (Luke 19:9–10). When Zacchaeus was accepted, he made changes to the way he was living and received what he may not have even known he needed, the approval of the Lord.

When our girls make the decision to love others well, to accept them no matter what their appearance, they also will find the approval of the Lord in a profound and powerful way. Why wouldn't we be praying for them to know and experience that?

In a world that says "Not you," may our girls be a reflection of the God who says, "You too!"

Prayers

Lord, may _____ have a love for others that is patient and kind. May she be quick to give the benefit of the doubt and never indulge the desire to keep score or be rude. (1 Corinthians 13:4–5)

Lord, You say love covers a multitude of sins. I pray _____ _____ will learn to walk in this truth, choosing to love even when it's hard, even when it hurts. May she love earnestly and sincerely, choosing not to give up or walk away when relationships get hard. (1 Peter 4:8)

Lord, I pray the love _____ has for people will continue to increase throughout her life. May she love better and deeper as she understands more and more the depths of Your love for her. (1 Thessalonians 3:12)

Lord, may _____ put on love every single day. No matter where she's going or what she's doing, may love for others be evident in her appearance and interactions. (Colossians 3:14)

Lord, I pray _____'s life will be fruitful in every way. May she exhibit love in all things and at all times, as Your Spirit teaches and guides her to live for You. I pray that the fruit of Your Spirit will be evident in every area of her life. (Galatians 5:22–23)

Lord, when others would give up, may _____ _____ have a love that endures. When relationships falter, when she's hurt by others, when she feels alone and let down, may she continue to love. And may her enduring love be a testimony to others of Your never-ending love for all of us. (Hebrews 13:1)

Lord, I pray _____ will have a passionate love for You. And even more, that her love for You will move her into a generous, overwhelming love for others, especially those who are lonely and in need. May her love for You motivate her to reach out to the ones others never even see. (James 1:27)

Lord, You say it's our love for others that best reveals our love for You. May _____ let that truth sink deep into her soul. May she love others fiercely and in a way that draws attention not to her, but to You. I pray that the way she loves will lead others to seek You. (John 13:35)

Lord, it's hard to love others the way we love ourselves. But that's what You've called us to do. I pray that _____ _____ will be willing to learn how to love this way, how to give others the same grace and kindness she would want for herself. (Mark 12:31)

Lord, if loving others were a competition, I pray _____ _____ would be passionate about winning. May she be on a mission to have a love that abounds more and more, to show others even just a taste of the great love You have for us. (Romans 12:10)

Just for Moms

I've felt the sting of "Not you" in my life more times than I care to admit. I've also felt the sting of social media updates that don't include me. How do we navigate those feelings inside us? For me, I've found it is most helpful to look around and see who else may be hearing "Not you."

As God reveals those people to me, I make a concerted effort to reach out to them and be a "You too" voice in their lives. If you are struggling with feeling left out, lonely, and isolated, maybe this is really an opportunity for you to find others who may be feeling the same way and invite them into your life.

Lord, we live in a "Not you" world. And there are times when we can be guilty of wallowing in our self-pity, our hurt feelings, and our left-outness. Forgive us when we can only see ourselves. Give us a desire to love others well, to see the ones around us who are also hearing the "Not you" message. May we be willing to step out of our comfort zones and reach out to others to say, "Hey! You too!" Let us be women who include when others would exclude, who encourage when others would ostracize, and who love when others would ignore. In Jesus' name, Amen.

Girl Talk

For little girls—Younger children are often more accepting than older ones. A great way to encourage a kind spirit as they age is to begin helping them see people who are lonely and unaccepted now. A simple way to do this is by visiting a local nursing home or elderly members of your church or community who are unable to get out and about. When Casiday was little, we often used holidays as an occasion to go visit the homebound in our church.

For "middle" girls—Ask your daughter about the children in her class at school or at church. Discuss who sits alone or doesn't seem to fit in. Encourage her to reach out to that person. Maybe she can ask the lonely girl to sit by her at lunch or in class. Or invite the one who doesn't fit in to join her group for an activity or a party. Talk with her about any times she has felt left out and how that made her feel. Share with her Proverbs 17:17 and talk about how she can be a loving friend to others.

For big girls—During this season of life, our daughters are likely to begin having friends who make far different choices than they do. Talk with your daughter about how to manage a relationship with a friend who is making choices with which she disagrees. Help her understand that loving someone doesn't mean agreeing with every choice they make. This is also a great time to develop a plan with her in case she finds herself in a situation where she is uncomfortable.

PART 5

Prayers for Her Purpose

We all have dreams and goals and hopes for our children. We want them to be happy, to have good friends, to marry well, and to have healthy families. We dream about what jobs they might have and hope they'll live close by so we can be active in our grandchildren's lives. And there really isn't anything wrong with any of that . . . as long as our first priority is a desire for them to live in the full purpose God has for them.

We must submit our desires to His plans and trust that what He has in store for them is far beyond what we could ever ask or imagine (Ephesians 3:20).

One of our most important jobs as moms is to partner with God in equipping and encouraging our girls to walk in His purposes, and also to get out of the way when He is working in them.

Salvation

May she come to saving knowledge of You
and be changed by Your love for her.

For "everyone who calls on the name of the Lord will be saved."

Romans 10:13

April 1, 2007: I was rushing around to get us to church on time. In the middle of looking for Casiday's socks and trying to figure out what to do with my hair, my sweet little seven-year-old said, "Mommy, I need to talk to you."

(Can I be really honest here? I was a little frantic thinking we didn't have time for a conversation about the latest baby-doll tragedy. But her face was determined, and I quickly decided it was better to spend three minutes listening now than taking the next thirty to explain why we didn't have time for me to listen now. Clearly I'd traveled this particular road before.)

We climbed into her daddy's big recliner, and she started sobbing. I mean SOBBING. I asked her what had happened as my mind played out every worst-case scenario a mom can conceive. Through her tears, she finally uttered these words, "I need saved."

Immediately tears filled my eyes as I looked at my precious daughter. As her crying slowed, we talked about what it means to be saved. After a few minutes of conversation, she looked at me with the most determined face and said, "I really need to pray. Right now."

We bowed our heads right there in that big old green recliner, and my daughter admitted her sin and confidently acknowledged Jesus as her Savior. As she thanked Him for loving her, my tears poured, and I added my own gratitude for answering my prayer for her salvation.

As soon as she said, "Amen," her demeanor changed. Where there had been desperation, I now saw certainty. Where there had been fear, I now recognized peace. I was watching 2 Corinthians 5:17: "Therefore, if anyone is in Christ, he is a new creation. The old has passed away; behold, the new has come."

We spent a few minutes discussing what it means to be saved and what God wanted her to do next. One of the things Scott and I have encouraged people to do upon making a profession of faith is to write it down. We know how the enemy wants us to question if our salvation really happened. Casiday quickly ran to her room and brought back her Bible and a pen. She scrawled these words, "April 1st 2007. I asked Jesus in my heart. JOY."

The Most Important Prayer

JOY indeed. As moms, the most important prayer we utter is for our children to be saved. I began praying for Casiday's salvation from the moment I knew I was pregnant. Of all the things I've prayed for my girl, my most desperate and urgent pleas were for her to be saved. Everything else paled in comparison to that request.

All the prayers we utter for their identity and hearts and minds and relationships begin in the hope of salvation. Our daughters can only walk in the fullness of their identity in Christ when they belong to Him. Their hearts and minds can only be rooted in and guided by Him when they have experienced salvation through Him. The way they relate to others can truly reflect the character of Christ only if they are being conformed to Him.

You may be thinking, if this is the most important prayer, why is it in the final part of the book? Honestly, I asked myself the same question as I worked on the outline. The prayers in this section are the hardest prayers we will pray. This is where the rubber meets the road, so to speak. This is where we take all those other desires and dreams we have for our girls and lay them down at the feet of Jesus. When we pray for their salvation, we recognize that they have a need that we as moms can never meet. We can't save them. And we can't be saved enough for them to inherit our salvation.

These prayers are at the end of the book because they are the beginning of the hard work we do after reading.

Letting Go and Letting God

You've seen the bumper sticker "Let go and let God," right? I hate it. It's pithy and trite and cliché. And while those are the reasons I'm annoyed by the saying, they aren't the reason I hate it. I hate it because it's hard, and I don't want to do it. Especially in regard to my daughter's spiritual growth.

I want a formula for success. I want to know that as long as we raise her in church, pray with her, give her excellent resources, and talk with her about her relationship with the Lord, she is going to be okay.

It doesn't work that way.

There comes a point when we are forced to accept that we cannot control our children's relationship with the Lord. We can point them to Jesus and share with them the truth of the Word, but ultimately, it is God who woos them to himself. And it is they who will make the choice to follow or walk away.

I'm not trying to be Debbie Downer. Really, it's a good thing. We pray for, nurture, and encourage our daughters to know the beauty of salvation. But we rest in the knowledge that it is not our work or words that accomplish salvation, it is the work on the cross of the Word-Made-Flesh. And we know this truth as well: As much as we desire our daughters to be saved, their heavenly Father desires it even more (1 Timothy 2:4; 2 Peter 3:9).

Casiday carried her Bible to church that Sunday morning in 2007 and proudly showed what she had written to countless people in our church. We called our families to share her good news. A few months later she was baptized by her daddy, who said, "I baptize you, my daughter and now my sister, in the name of the Father and the Son and the Holy Spirit."

My daughter and my sister. That's what she is now. Truly, *joy* is the word.

PRAYERS

Lord, I pray _____ will recognize her need for salvation early in life and call upon Your name, knowing it is only through You any of us can be saved. (Acts 2:21, Joel 2:32)

Lord, You alone are the means of our salvation, the hope of our redemption. I pray _____ will find her hope and security in You, knowing it is You who offer her redemption. (Acts 4:12)

Lord, I'm thankful You are the One who saves "to the uttermost" and for the invitation You give that we may draw near to You. May _____ find peace in Your presence and know You are always interceding on her behalf before the Father. (Hebrews 7:25)

Lord, You came to pay the price for our sins. You are the ransom, what was necessary for our salvation. My fervent prayer is for _____ to grasp the sweetness of salvation, the grace of Your life given for ours. (Mark 10:45)

Lord, it's so hard sometimes to wait for _____ to know You, to live in the fullness of life You offer. Give me the strength to wait for You to move in her. Remind me that her salvation can come only from You; I can't do this for her. (Psalm 62:1)

Lord, may _____ be bold and willing to confess with her mouth that You ARE Lord. May she believe that You have defeated death, and because You now live, she can have eternal life. (Romans 10:9)

Lord, I pray _____ will never believe the lie that she's not worthy of Your salvation. May she know that she doesn't have to clean herself up before she comes to You. Help her grasp the truth that while we were still sinners, You died for us. (Romans 5:7–8)

Lord, I'm thankful You desire for all to come to a saving knowledge of You. I know this is Your plan for _____ _____. May I trust Your timing in this and in all things, ever aware that Your love for her far exceeds my own. (2 Peter 3:9)

Lord, may _____ know there is nothing she can do to earn her salvation. She doesn't have to be good enough and, in truth, she could never be good enough. Teach her to see the gift of grace, the favor You bestow upon her. May she have faith to trust You and rest in the work You have already done. (Ephesians 2:8–9)

Lord, You came to seek out and save the lost. I pray _____ _____ will trust You with her heart and life, knowing You have sought her out and long for a relationship with her. (Luke 19:10)

Just for Moms

My first and most important prayer for Casiday was that she would be saved. And, I imagine that if you're reading this, you have that same desire for your daughter. But there may come a day when your child says she isn't sure she's really saved. Or maybe you'll wonder the same thing.

One Wednesday night when she was in seventh grade, Casiday told me she wasn't sure about her salvation. Having had some doubts of my own when I was in my early twenties, I shared my own story with her. And then I pointed her back to truth. We pulled out her Bible and read what she had written. We looked up Romans 10:9 and read it together, talking about what it meant.

We had these conversations a few times over the course of a month or so. Ultimately, Casiday came to the conclusion that she had confessed that Jesus was Lord and believed that God raised Him from the dead when she prayed that Sunday morning in 2007. But perhaps you are still struggling with some doubt.

First, I urge you to talk with your pastor or a mature godly woman in your church. Share your doubts and ask them to pray for you to have clarity. Second, ask your questions. There is nothing wrong with wanting to make sure you are truly saved. Third, trust the Word above your feelings. Read Romans 10:9 and Ephesians 2:8–9. These Scriptures make it clear that our salvation is based on confession of Christ and belief He is Lord. We can't do enough or be good enough to earn our salvation; it's based on the grace of God through faith.

And if your daughter ever comes to you with doubts, listen with tenderness and grace. Offer her the truth of the Word. Don't stress out! It is God's desire for all to be saved, and if He is at work in her, He will reveal himself in a manner she can understand.

Lord, we all face seasons when doubt comes easier than faith. It can be easy for us to start thinking we must do more or be more in order to earn our salvation. Help us trust Your Word. Give us the courage to believe it is You who has done the work. Like the man who sought healing for his son, we sometimes pray, "I believe. Help my unbelief." Thank You for meeting us where we are. Give us wisdom and understanding to work through our doubts. Help us not to be too prideful to ask for others to pray for us and help us find the answers in Scripture. For our daughters who aren't saved, Lord, we pray You will draw them to You. Make Your love for them unavoidable. And when our daughters struggle with doubts of their own, we pray for wisdom to guide them back to You. In Jesus' name, Amen.

Girl Talk

As I mentioned, these are the most important prayers we pray for our girls. Which means that these are also the most important conversations we have with them.

For little girls—Ask your daughter if she knows what sin is. Explain that we all are sinners and how Jesus saves us. My favorite method for sharing the plan of salvation with younger children is ABC. A is for accept. We must first accept that we are sinners and we need a Savior. B is for believe. After we recognize our need for a Savior, we must believe Jesus is the Savior. C is for confess. Romans 10:9–10 tells us that if we confess and believe, we will be saved. Don't pressure your daughter to make any decision until she is ready. More than anything, you want to make sure she understands the truth about salvation.

For "middle" girls—By this stage, it is possible your daughter has already made a profession of faith in Christ and been baptized. Share with her your own salvation story, and, if you haven't already, this is a great time to have her write down when she was saved and the details she wants to remember. If she hasn't yet come to salvation, use the ABC method (above) to share with her.

For big girls—As I mentioned, Casiday was young when she was saved, and when she was a little older, she had some doubts. It's likely your daughter, if she was saved as a young child, is having some doubts. Open the door for her to share those concerns or fears with you. Walk her through Romans 10:9–10. Share your salvation story and talk about any times you have also doubted. If you sense she may not be certain of her salvation, that's okay too. Give her some space to process and have another conversation in a few days. If she determines she hasn't been saved, it is such a gift to lead her to the Lord. (The ABC method noted above can be used no matter how old the person is.) If she's certain of her salvation, encourage her to write about her confidence and to add the date. Tell her she can always come back and read it when she faces other seasons of doubt.

19

Sanctification

May she embrace the process of being conformed to Your image, sanctified by You.

But as he who called you is holy, you also be holy in all your conduct.

1 Peter 1:15

I really had no idea what I was asking God for when I prayed this prayer:

Watch over my baby, Lord. Because the truth is, as much as I love her and desire good things for her, You love her more and better . . . and Your plan for her is good. This year, my prayer for her is that she will grasp hold of the truth that You are all she really needs and that she will spend the rest of her life clinging to the hope that truth gives.[1]

Casiday's sophomore year was awful. And, somehow, I feel as though my sincere but unknowing prayer may have been partly responsible. It sounds so good, doesn't it, to pray that our girls will learn that Jesus is all they really need? Let me assure you there is a big difference between the beauty of those words on a page and the harsh reality of those words lived out in your girl's life. And it is achingly hard to watch.

By the end of the school year, my girl had decided not to try out for cheerleading, broken up with her boyfriend, and could count on one hand the number of friends she really had. She had cried more tears than I thought possible, made a few really poor decisions, and spent a whole lot of time by herself.

As a mom, I wanted to fix it all. (And I may have had to bite my tongue a few times so I didn't make some situations worse.) In no way am I implying my daughter is somehow better than anyone else. On the contrary, she is incredibly normal. Much of the sorrow and struggle she had that year were attributable to a nasty combination of hormones, insecurity, and personality. It wasn't always pretty. And it definitely wasn't always fun.

But, even on the worst days, one thing remained true: God is good. It was His goodness at work in her, rooting out the parts of her character that didn't reflect His.

Pruning Hurts

For the record, I'm not very good with plants. I have a gardenia Scott's grandmother gave me. She rooted it from a clipping off a gardenia bush her mother had. Basically, I do really well with it at the beginning of summer, and then it gets hot and I forget about it (and all the other flowers I plant every year), so it turns all brown and dead-looking. I look at it with sad eyes and then cut off all the dead parts. And something amazing happens—within a few weeks I begin to see tiny hints of green peeking out. What looked worthless and dead now has signs of life.

Cutting away the dead parts is called pruning. And Jesus said it has to happen in the lives of believers just like it does in plants.

> "Every branch in me that does not bear fruit he takes away, and every branch that does bear fruit he prunes, that it may bear more fruit."
>
> John 15:2

My gardenia doesn't cry out when I start clipping away on it. But people tend to be more vocal when we are being spiritually pruned because, well, it hurts. When God starts stripping away all the unnecessary parts, all the unhealthy relationships, all the life-draining mess, we feel the rip. And we don't always recognize it as being His good work in us. In fact, most of the time we don't realize what was really happening until we can look back.

Partnering in Sanctification

Pruning is part of the work the Holy Spirit does in the life of a believer. We know it's necessary, but that doesn't mean we like it while it happens. I didn't recognize how God was using my prayer in Casiday's life until I sat down to write a prayer over her junior year. As I read what I'd written the year before, I could see how God had faithfully answered my request. But it certainly didn't look like what I'd expected (or wanted).

What mom wants to see her daughter deal with rejection or insecurity or isolation? Not this one! And I'm guessing not the ones reading this either.

So what do we do when our girls are being pruned? When every instinct in us would stop the work God is doing, how can we instead partner with Him to accomplish His purpose for her? In John 15, we find a few important truths.

We must trust God's love. In verses 12–15, Jesus speaks of the love He has for us, the love that lays down its life for friends. When our girls are facing hard seasons, we must remember that the depth of God's love for them surpasses even our own. And because of that knowledge, we can trust His sanctifying work in their lives.

We must abide in Him ourselves. Jesus invites us to know the fruit-bearing life He brings as we abide in Him (verses 4, 7). Asking our girls to trust God's work in their lives when we are not living it out in our own is a recipe for disaster. Our daughters need to see us walking with the Lord, and, especially as they get older, they need us to share our own seasons of pruning with them.

We must acknowledge His authority in their lives. This is the hardest part: admitting that God has greater authority and power in their lives than we do. We have to step back so He can accomplish His purpose in them. Jesus reminds us, "Apart from me you can do nothing" (verse 5). Our girls need to see us affirming the work God does in them, even the hard parts. They need us to remember for ourselves and remind them it is His power that gives them power, not anything we as moms can do for them.

We want our girls to know the certainty of being saved. But we also know salvation doesn't bring the easy life. Jesus said, "In the world you will have tribulation. But take heart; I have overcome the world" (John 16:33). Our girls will experience the hard days of life. They will know heartbreak and suffering. We pray for their salvation urgently so they will also know the peace that transcends all understanding (Philippians 4:7) when life brings storms.

So here we sit, a year removed from what, so far, was the hardest year of my girl's life. I don't know all the ways those experiences and heartaches will affect the days ahead. But I do know this: my prayer was answered. God absolutely helped her grab the truth that He is all she needs, that all her hope can be placed in Him. Will she lose sight of that sometimes? Probably. But this I know: she's His, and He will continue to prune her, sanctify her, and draw her closer to Him for the rest of her life. And I'll continue to pray for those very things.

PRAYERS

Lord, I pray _____ will rest in the knowledge that she is made in Your image and You will do the work of completing what You have begun in her. (Philippians 1:6)

Lord, as _____ grasps the beauty of who she is in You, may she also be filled with a desire to pursue holiness. (1 Peter 1:15)

Lord, may _____ desire to be transformed into Your image, to walk in the glory of Your likeness. May she humble herself before You, allowing You to mold her life into what You would have her be. (2 Corinthians 3:18)

Lord, thank You for the sweet truth that in You we are made new. All the old is gone, the new has come. I pray _____ will find great comfort and confidence in this assurance. (2 Corinthians 5:17)

Lord, sanctification isn't easy. I don't look forward to watching You do the hard work of molding _____ into Your image, but I trust You to do what is necessary. May she also trust You, longing to receive the outcome of her faith, believing in You and knowing the joy that comes from walking with You. (1 Peter 1:8–9)

Lord, You save us for a holy calling. It's Your purpose and grace that move us into a closer relationship with You. May _____ be open to Your movement in her life and willing to submit to the pruning You will do. (2 Timothy 1:9)

Lord, when _____ has wandered from Your presence, may she hear Your voice calling her. I pray she will bend her heart toward You, knowing You are gracious and merciful, slow to anger, and abounding in love. (Joel 2:13)

Lord, I pray _____ will be wise, knowing how to discern truth from falsehood. Give her insight to test what she hears and know what is from You and what is not. (1 John 4:1)

Lord, thank You for hearing us when we cry out to You. May _____ know that You are her Deliverer, that You are near when she is hurting, and that You are close when her spirit is crushed. (Psalm 34:17–18)

Lord, just as Paul understood the sufferings of this world are "not worth comparing" to the glory You will one day reveal, I pray _____ will not allow the hardships and trials of this life to overshadow the hope and joy she has in You. (Romans 8:18)

Just for Moms

Maybe it isn't your girl but you who is experiencing a season of sanctification. Oh, friend, I get it. As my girl's junior year began, those holy pruning shears got ahold of me. I felt every cut as God stripped away some relationships and forced some truths I didn't want to see to the surface. Pruning isn't easy when you're fifteen, and it's not any easier when you're forty-five. But when I quit resisting and chose to trust that the work was necessary, I was reminded of how precious that sanctifying work can be. As He cuts away the unnecessary parts, what is left is far more beautiful.

Lord, sanctification isn't fun. And pruning hurts. When You start stripping away all the walls we've built, all the masks we wear, the vulnerability feels overwhelming. We feel exposed, bare, and ugly. Help us remember the pruning is for our good, to make us more like You. When it hurts and we think it will never end, remind us of Your love that heals and never ends. Teach us to abide in You and trust Your Holy Spirit's work in us. Prune us to bear much fruit for Your glory. In Jesus' name, Amen.

Girl Talk

For little girls—Set aside time to make cookies together. Be sure to make a kind requiring a cookie cutter. As you are cutting out the cookies, explain how Jesus wants us to look like Him. Just like the cookie cutter separates the extra dough from the cookie, God works in us to remove the parts that don't look like Him.

For "middle" girls—Around this age, many girls get braces. Talk with your daughter about how braces work to align the teeth, and make note that it isn't a quick process. Share with her 1 Peter 1:15 and explain God's desire for us to be holy. Explain to her the process of becoming holy is often called sanctification. Using Philippians 1:6, remind her that our sanctification takes our whole lives but will be complete when we meet Jesus in heaven.

For big girls—Gather up photos of your daughter from the time she was a baby until now. Look over them together and make note of all the ways she has changed. Explain that we also change spiritually as we mature in Christ in the process of sanctification. Talk with her about some of the ways God has worked this process in your life and even some ways you have noticed Him at work in her. Ask her if she can identify areas where God may be working during this season. Share Philippians 1:6 with her as a reminder that the sanctification process takes our whole lives but will be complete in Christ.

20

Steadfast

May she choose to live steadfastly for
you, even when she may stand alone.

Abide in me, and I in you. As the branch cannot bear fruit by
itself, unless it abides in the vine, neither can you, unless you
abide in me.

John 15:4

Walk with me," she said. "I want to talk with you about
something."

I joined my sixty-six-year-old friend, curious about what she
would say. As we meandered away from the rest of the senior
adult group, happily enjoying the cool breeze and beautiful
foliage of the Smoky Mountains in the fall, Mrs. Lois began
speaking.

"I know it's hard for you sometimes. Raising a child, serving with Scott, and everything else you do. I want you to know I think you are doing a great job."

She stopped speaking and I mumbled my thanks, trying not to cry. It had been awhile since I'd felt like I was doing a good job at anything. My friend grabbed my hand and we kept walking, my tears falling onto the bright leaves along our path.

After a few minutes of the quiet, we reached a bench and Mrs. Lois moved to it and sat down, patting the seat beside her. As I sat down, she turned to me and said, "I love you. And I'm proud to know you. But I need to say something, and it won't be easy for me to say, and it will be hard for you to hear."

I sucked in a deep breath, uncertain of what this kind woman who had loved me so well was about to say.

"You know so much about the Bible," she began. "I'm amazed at how deep your love for the Word of God is, and the way you share the truth and encourage others is just beautiful. But, Teri Lynne, you need to learn to believe it is all true for you. All those things you tell others, about how Jesus loves them as they are, about how God is for them, about how they can depend on Him? My heart hurts because I see how much you struggle to accept all of that truth in your own life."

That crisp autumn day God used a precious woman I adored to break me. The breaking wasn't to destroy me, of course (though it may have felt that way at the time). God allowed Mrs. Lois to see something in my life that, left unchecked, would have destroyed me.

He's like that, you know, always working for our good even when we can't see it (Romans 8:28). After that trip, one word captivated me, a word I'd heard my whole life, a word I'd studied and heard preached countless times.

Abide.

Though I'd heard it, I'd never grasped it. Until then.

Abide in Me

In John 15, Jesus explains what it means to abide in Him. Take a moment now and read verses 4 through 10. In these verses, Jesus outlines three ways we must abide in Him, and He shares what we gain when we do abide.

1. Abide in His Presence (verses 4–5)

We had a large group of friends in Georgia that we referred to as our "framily." Rarely was there a Sunday afternoon when at least one or two of them were not in our home. And you could almost always find someone taking a Sunday nap somewhere. I love that our home was a place where people could rest. No need for me to entertain or for them to feel pressured to carry a conversation. There is a sweetness found simply by being in the presence of those who love and accept us.

Jesus offers us that same sweet acceptance when we choose to abide in Him. We receive the gift of His presence, sure and steady. And we are invited to come as we are, weary and worried, tired and torn, He welcomes us. Just as God promised His presence would both go with the Israelites and provide them rest (Exodus 33:14), we can be sure of Christ's willingness to be with us always as we abide in Him.

2. Abide in His Word (verse 7)

Mrs. Lois knew I knew the Bible. But she also understood there is a huge difference between knowing something and living something. I wasn't living what I knew. I wasn't abiding in His Word.

Jesus said, "If you abide in me, and my words abide in you, ask whatever you wish, and it will be done for you" (John 15:7). What a powerful promise! Since that long-ago conversation with

Mrs. Lois, I've learned an important truth: When we abide in His Word, when we truly allow it to soak into our hearts and minds and transform our lives, the whatevers we wish for are changed. We seek His kingdom, not ours. We long for His fame, not ours. We want His will, not ours. We grasp the words of John the Baptist, "He must increase, but I must decrease" (John 3:30).

3. Abide in His love (verses 9–10)

Whenever I think about God's love, I can't help but consider these words of Paul—his desire that the Ephesians "may have strength to comprehend with all the saints what is the breadth and length and height and depth, and to know the love of Christ that surpasses knowledge, that you may be filled with all the fullness of God" (Ephesians 3:18–19).

Jesus wants us to know His love for us is as sure as the Father's love for His Son. Just as God loves Christ, so Christ loves us. Is there anything more comforting than to rest in the certainty of God's unfathomable love?

Result of Abiding

"By this my Father is glorified, that you bear much fruit and so prove to be my disciples."

John 15:8

Jesus says two things happen when we abide in Him: we bear fruit and God gets the glory. What more could we ever want for ourselves and for our girls? In 1 John 2:6 we read, "Whoever says he abides in him ought to walk in the same way in which he walked."

John writes of walking in the same way Jesus walked as the evidence of knowing we are abiding in Christ. How do we know how He walked? The primary source we have for understanding the way of Christ is Scripture. Spending daily time in both study and meditation on the Bible is necessary to our spiritual growth. We cannot grow in Christ without a commitment to time in His Word.

But simply reading the Bible isn't enough.

Read James 1:22–27. In these verses we see a clear imperative: We must act on what we read. Just as an encounter with Christ changes us, so too should our time in the Word transform us and conform us to Him.

Bearing fruit is the result of an intentional and disciplined choice to spend time with the Lord and put into action what we learn from Him and His Word. Bearing fruit is the primary purpose of all creation (see Genesis 1:11–12, 22, 28) and in our redemption (John 15:8, 16). We are called to bear fruit, and in order to do so we must first learn to abide.

Our girls will need us to help them understand all of this and to guide them as they learn to be steadfast in their faith. There will be seasons when abiding isn't easy or even when they don't want to do it. In those times, we can share our own stories of walking steadfastly, of abiding. And, we get to remind them of the great joy we all have when we point others toward the Lord, no matter what our circumstances.

I'm thankful Mrs. Lois chose to speak those honest words into my life. She loves me and wants to see God's best for and in me. As moms, we need to follow Mrs. Lois' example and be willing to speak truth into our girls with love and grace.

Prayers

Lord, I pray _____ will be steadfast and immovable. May she know her life and actions for Your kingdom are valuable when she seeks Your glory through them. (1 Corinthians 15:58)

Lord, may _____ long for a deeper relationship with You. May she "taste and see" that You are good and continue to grow in You for her whole life. (1 Peter 2:2, Psalm 34:8)

Lord, our relationships with You are deeply personal, but they are never meant to be private. The world will try to tell her it's okay to believe, but she mustn't act on her beliefs. I pray_____ won't be deceived but will stand for You, willing both to speak and to act at Your prompting. (James 1:22)

Lord, just as Job was certain of his faith in the midst of unbearable tragedy, I pray _____ will know the assurance that You live and one day will stand upon the earth, making all things once again right and new. (Job 19:25)

Lord, may _____ be wise to recognize the thief, the one who wants only to steal, kill, and destroy. May she stand against his schemes and walk in confidence, sure of the abundant life You have purposed and planned for her. (John 10:10)

Lord, I pray _____ will heed Your instructions, knowing she will stay on the path to true life as she walks with You. May she be faithful to accept correction and mindful to point others toward You. (Proverbs 10:17)

Lord, when she is weary from life, when she wants to give up, when it all seems too hard, may _____ remember You daily bear her up. May she praise You always, recognizing You are her salvation and her hope. (Psalm 68:19)

Lord, the days will come when _____ wonders if she's good enough, if You can really love her. As much as I wish she would never face those hard times, I know they are necessary. It's those days of emptiness, of wondering, when she will truly find there is nothing that can separate her from Your faithful, unending, certain love. (Romans 8:38–39)

Lord, Your eyes are looking for those who are faithful, who remain upright and steadfast even in the midst of an ungodly culture. I pray _____ will be one who pursues a life that is holy. And as she lives in that manner, may she know the certainty of Your support and protection. (2 Chronicles 16:9)

Lord, it can be hard for _____ to imagine that one day she'll stand before You and give an account of her life. But Your Word says we will all do just that. I pray, even now, she will begin setting her course on the path that is straight and narrow so she can hear those precious words, "Well done, good and faithful servant. . . . Enter into the joy of your master." (Matthew 25:21)

Just for Moms

I wish I could say I've always heeded the wise counsel Mrs. Lois gave me. I haven't. In the years since we sat on that bench, there have been days and weeks when I've failed to abide in Christ, when I've resisted allowing His Word to penetrate deep inside me.

Sometimes it's been because I'm angry, other times it's been rooted in disappointment, and sometimes I've just been lazy. Maybe you need someone to speak truth into your life right now, just like I did then. Can I echo Mrs. Lois's words to you?

Friend, you need to learn to believe all the words you pray for your girl, and that what you tell her about God's love and plan for her are also true for you!

Lord, it's so easy for us to know what Your Word says and to believe it for others. But sometimes we have a very difficult time believing it for ourselves. Somehow we convince ourselves that of all the people in the world, we're the only ones not worthy of Your love and grace. It's a lie, a terrible but powerful lie our enemy loves to weave into our thoughts. Will You give us the boldness to believe You and trust Your Word when the enemy attacks us? Will You help us come with confidence before Your throne, knowing we belong there and that we have access to the King of kings and Lord of lords? Give us courage to walk steadfastly in You. May our hearts' desire be to abide in You, that we can bear fruit for Your kingdom and that You would receive all the glory. In Jesus' name, Amen.

Girl Talk

For little girls—Read 2 Kings 5:1–14. In this story we see a young servant girl who knew about God and shared His healing power with another person. Use this story to help your daughter see that she is never too young to help others see Jesus.

For "middle" girls—Share with your daughter what God is teaching you now as you study His Word. Ask her what she is learning in her Bible study, Sunday school class, or youth group.

Talk about ways each of you could put into practice what you have learned. Together, make a plan to act on what you know.

For big girls—Using the same idea as for "middle" girls, share with your daughter what each of you are learning about God and His desires for your life. But also share with her a time when you knew what He would have you do but chose not to be obedient. Talk with her about how important it is to act on what you know.

Share

May she have an urgency to share the Good News of Your love and salvation with others.

And he said to them, "Go into all the world and proclaim the gospel to the whole creation."

Mark 16:15

On Monday nights from April through September, something special happens in our little north Alabama town. A bunch of high school and college students play in a park with the children who live in nearby government housing.

Swings are pushed while children laugh and cry out, "Higher, higher." A group of four tosses a foam football and laughs when it's dropped by one of the adults present. Others play basketball on the concrete slab where the hoop with a metal net hangs and clangs with every shot.

Once everyone is good and sweaty, they all gather in the graffiti-covered pavilion where one of the leaders or an invited guest shares a short Bible lesson.

Teenagers sit with kindergarteners, gently reminding them not to talk when someone else is talking. College students count out plates and juice boxes. Adults settle in between boys who aren't always good at keeping their hands to themselves.

It doesn't look like anything remarkable. In fact, I'd imagine most people driving by wouldn't even notice. Actually, Eastside Park isn't a place most people drive by anyway.

I bet there are places like this in your town too. Ugly places where the most beautiful things are happening. Dry places where the Living Water is being shared. Hopeless places where the truest hope is proclaimed.

Sometimes we forget, don't we, how simple it can be to share the gospel? We think about all the reasons we can't "go ye therefore"—finances and fear probably topping most of our lists.

Maybe you can't go to the uttermost. You know what? It's okay! God has called us all to go, we just need to be willing to go as far as He leads. For some of us, that means we'll engage in local missions with a passion; for others, it may be a call to a lifetime of living in another country. For many, it will be a combination of many different places and ways in the various seasons of our lives.

Our job as moms in this area is twofold: pray and prepare.

Pray. As scary as it is, we need to pray that our girls will be open to whatever task the Lord calls them to, wherever He leads. Which also means that we need to pray that He will give us the willingness to surrender our girls to obey. (I know. That is the hard part, right?)

Prepare. Not only must we pray for their hearts to be willing, we must give them the tools they need to prepare them for whatever He asks of them. We do this by showing them a life of faithful service, by inviting them to join us as we share the gospel, by opening their eyes to the countless ways we can go and tell the Good News.

Several years ago, Scott and I had the great privilege to go to Roatán, Honduras, on a mission trip. He preached in local churches, and I led women's Bible studies. But most of what we did was the same thing we can do right here in our little north Alabama town—we loved people. We didn't build any new churches, but we built up the pastors and missionaries who needed encouragement. We didn't feed thousands, but we did carry meals to precious elderly women who had prayed for years over their poor city, aware the poverty was spiritual even more than material.

We played with children at orphanages, pushing them on swings and kicking soccer balls. And it looked a whole lot like what happens every Monday at Eastside.

Our girls need us to show them by example that we share our faith best by living it out among the least.

PRAYERS

Lord, may _____ understand the urgency of the gospel. I pray she will be diligent to share Your love and the hope of salvation with others. May she walk in the power of Your Spirit at work in her and be a powerful witness of Your faithfulness and grace. (Acts 1:8)

Lord, just as _____ knows her sins have been blotted out by Christ's blood, may she be faithful to tell others of Your salvation that is available to all. May she share the redemption she has received and invite others to know the peace You offer. (Isaiah 44:22)

Lord, when You sent Your Son, it was for all of us. I pray _____ knows the power of the love You displayed and that she will tell others of the eternal life You have made available to them. (John 3:16)

Lord, may _____ have the beautiful feet that spread the gospel, tell the Good News, and remind others of the salvation and peace available in You. (Isaiah 52:7, Romans 10:15)

Lord, I pray _____ will be wide open to whatever You ask her to do. May she go to the nations, proclaiming the gospel. And give me the wisdom to let her go, trusting that Your plans for her are far better than anything I could dream up. (Mark 16:15)

Lord, I pray the day comes when people will ask _____ the same question the Philippian jailer asked Paul and Silas: "What must I do to be saved?" And when they ask, give her boldness and confidence to share the hope we have in the cross. (Acts 16:30–31)

Lord, as hard as this is for me to consider, I do pray that _____ will be willing to lose her life for Your sake. May she love You more than she loves anything or anyone in this world, and realize it is only in You that we can experience true life. (Matthew 16:25)

Lord, may _____ say, as Isaiah did, "Here am I, Lord. Send me!" May she have a heart for the lost and a passion to share the gospel with others. May her prayer every day be, "Send me." (Isaiah 6:8)

Lord, I pray _____ will never be ashamed of the gospel, never shrink from sharing what You have done for her, never back down from telling others the way to salvation. May her faith be bold and unwavering. (Romans 1:16–17)

Lord, I pray _____ will know she has authority in You to go and tell others what You have done. May she be a disciple maker, and may she know that You are with her always, until the day of Your return. (Matthew 28:18–20)

Just for Moms

I'm not a regular at Eastside. Neither is my girl. But I serve every month at a free medical clinic for the uninsured in our area. Since Casiday wants to be a nurse, she often goes with me and observes with one of the nurses. When we lived in Georgia, I volunteered in several capacities with the local crisis pregnancy center. Before she started school, Casiday spent a lot of Thursday mornings coloring in the center's workroom while I met with clients.

I share all of that to say that the call on our lives to share may look different for each of us and, honestly, can often look different in our own lives at various times. May I encourage you with this: invite your girl, even your little girl, to join you in whatever you're doing. Did three-year-old Casiday understand what I was talking about with the clients at the pregnancy center? I sure hope not! But she saw me giving time and energy to serve others and to tell them about Jesus. Our girls want to be where we are. Take advantage of that desire and help them see all the ways we can share about the love of God with others.

Lord, I pray You will always open our eyes to see those in need of You. Give us boldness to speak of Your love. Help us show our girls what it is to share the gospel, to be light in the darkness of this world. When we're nervous, calm our hearts. When we're uncertain, give us peace. When we're afraid, give us faith. Make us into women who serve and share and sacrifice for Your sake. We want to raise daughters who will have bold faith and willing hearts. So give us bold faith and willing hearts as we live out Your love in our homes, our churches, our communities, and around the world. In Jesus' name and for His sake, Amen.

Girl Talk

For little girls—I asked the Prayers for Girls community for ideas about how to serve with their girls. Several of the moms with younger daughters shared how they help in local ministries. Even little girls can help serve and share Jesus in many ways. Some of my favorite suggestions include visiting a nursing home, helping prepare food baskets for those in need, and baking cookies for neighbors. Talk with your daughter about a way you two can serve together, and make a plan for doing it.

For "middle" girls—As our girls get older, the ways they can share Jesus' love with others can increase. Talk with your daughter about how you two could serve together. Ask for her ideas. And also discuss what opportunities she has to reflect the love of God in the places she already goes, like school, ball practices, and dance classes.

For big girls—Have an honest conversation with your daughter about the value of being intentional about sharing the gospel and Christ's love with others. As with "middle" girls, discuss ways you can serve together and also ask her for ideas for how she can share within the context of what she already does. Encourage her to remember that she needs to be available, but the results are in God's hands.

22

A Little Bit of Coffee and a Whole Lot of Jesus

I f you were to stop by my house around 6:30 in the morning, you'd most often find me with coffee in one of my favorite mugs, listening to the Ronnie Freeman station on Pandora, Bible and journal laid out, ready for my time in the Word. I sit there at the beautiful table-turned-desk my husband refinished for me, and I try to quiet all those whispers and shouts in my head. (I call them "the committee" because they all have something to say, and they never agree.) In the quiet of the moment I wait, because I'm learning that the best way to quiet my anxious heart is to still my body and trust God to still my heart and mind as I wait on Him.

As I sip on my coffee and make a list in my journal (which I should confess isn't so much a pretty journal as it is a five-subject notebook—I don't want you to have any grandiose ideas about that!), the list would look pretty random to most people. Names and tasks, those things weighing on me that I need to let go.

Once the list is finished, I pull out the Prayers for Girls calendar and look up the verse for that day's prayer. Carefully writing the verse in my journal/notebook, I take time to think about what it says. I read the verses around it and consider the context. And then I write a prayer for my girl.

By this point, she's usually sitting across from me. We have a seven o'clock appointment on school mornings, a shared quiet time. Some mornings we talk or pray together. But most of the time she reads while I'm reading, and then she quietly makes her way back to her room to finish getting ready for the day.

I'm not going to lie, there are a lot of days when I have to re-read whatever I was reading while she was there with me. The sight of her, Bible open, underlining in her devotional, eyes closed in prayer, well, it just leaves me undone.

As she walks past me, headed out the door for school, she stops and gives me a hug and kiss. I always say the same thing: "Have a good day. Be sweet. I love you!" She always replies, "I love you too!" And as she walks out the door, I remind her to be careful driving. I can hear her laugh as the door closes.

It's a nice little routine we have going. I'm thankful for it. But here's the thing: It's taken us a long time to get here. I drove her to school until this year, her junior year. And I'd love for you to believe our time in the car every morning was full of encouraging words and heartfelt prayers. But it usually wasn't.

There have been a lot of hard-fought battles over the past sixteen years. A lot. I've said words I deeply regret. She's done things she wishes she hadn't.

Parenting is hard. Parenting isn't for wimps, right? This mom gig is the hardest thing I've ever done, and even though we can see that the end of her days in our home are approaching far more quickly than we'd like, I'm still not sure how much I have done well.

This is what I know: I love her. My heart has always been to point her toward Jesus. I've prayed and I've guided. I've lectured and I've laughed. I've stayed awake at night praying the fevers would go down, and I've prayed her through hard days at high school.

Of all the lessons I've learned, this one stands out: Prayer changes me. Every time. When I pray for her to love the Lord, He shows me how to love Him more. When I pray for her to have a pure heart, He reveals the areas I need to confess. When I pray for her to have a renewed mind, He gives me a new focus and passion for Him. When I pray for her to be loving in her relationships, He helps me learn to love others better. And when I pray for her to walk in the purpose He has for her, He points me toward the purpose He has for me as well.

Praying is a gift. Do we pray for perfect daughters? Well, sure! Because wouldn't that be awesome. But really, deep inside, we pray for them because we know they don't have perfect moms. And we know that God alone can fill in all those glaring gaps in us. We know how much our girls need Him because we know how much we need Him.

I have a fun little sign hanging on the gallery wall in my office. It has the popular saying, "All I need is a little bit of coffee and a whole lot of Jesus." I love it because it reminds me of an important truth: I will always need more of what Jesus can do and less of what I can do myself. I can't parent her fueled by coffee (trust me, I tried when she was a baby and she was up every three hours). I can't parent her by what the books say or even by what works for others. I can only parent her through the grace and love of Christ.

He is all I really need.

And, my friend, He's all you really need too.

A PRAYER FOR YOU

Lord, thank You for the beautiful mom reading this prayer. I don't know what her circumstances are, what she's doing right, and where she feels like she's failing. But I know this: You know her. You see her. And You love her! You've placed in her a deep passion for praying for her daughter. We know that comes from You, and we thank You for it. Right now, Lord, I pray You will meet her wherever she is with a deep peace and awareness of Your presence. Will You draw her close and whisper Your tender love and care over her?

Give her the wisdom to parent her daughter, and give her grace to deal with herself. Help her remember that her prayers are weighty and good. Remind her that she is fighting for her daughter, and that she is not alone. Grant her insight to know how and what to pray and plant in her an abiding passion for Your Word. May her prayers become a strong foundation for her family. I pray her daughter will see the testimony of this mom and know Your faithfulness. Lord, I pray that one day her children will rise up and call her blessed. I pray the legacy she leaves will be one of mighty prayer and abiding faith. May Your strength be magnified in her weaknesses, and may she know the profound sufficiency of Your grace. In Jesus' name, Amen.

23

P.S. A Note to the Mom Who Is Struggling

My dear friend,

I know you are in the middle of some hard, hard days, and I want you to know, I get it! Sometimes we do all we know to do and still feel lost, wondering if we've failed, and ready to give up. From me to you: I understand. And it's really okay to feel this way.

Because no matter how we feel, our feelings can never outweigh God's truth and sovereignty in our lives. NEVER.

I've felt the weight of failure. I've doubted God's goodness for me and for my girl. I've watched her struggle with rejection and fear and anxiety. And I've wrestled with those same issues in my own life.

But this I know: God is faithful. Even when I can't see it, even when I don't understand. He is faithful. He can't not be!

I shared previously about Casiday's sophomore year. Nothing came easily. She lost a lot of friends. She made a few poor choices. She learned some incredibly hard lessons. And it was awful. I hated watching her go through it all. I hated knowing that some of it was the consequence of her own behavior. I hated not being able to make it all better. And most of all, I hated that it didn't seem to push her closer to the Lord; some days it seemed to push her farther away.

It was heartbreaking, and I felt absolutely helpless. More than once I wanted to scream at God, and more than once I found I couldn't pray. The ache in my heart led to a lump in my throat, and the words just wouldn't come. During those months, Habakkuk 3:17–19 became the song of my heart.

> Though the fig tree should not blossom,
>   nor fruit be on the vines,
> the produce of the olive fail
>   and the fields yield no food,
> the flock be cut off from the fold
>   and there be no herd in the stalls,
> yet I will rejoice in the Lord;
>   I will take joy in the God of my salvation.
> God, the Lord, is my strength;
>   he makes my feet like the deer's;
>   he makes me tread on my high places.

Habakkuk was writing to a people who were on the verge of losing everything. And he said, "Yet I will rejoice." Why? Because God is our salvation and our strength. Those verses carried me through when I wasn't sure I would make it.

Maybe you're in a hard season, or maybe your girl is in a battle of her own and you ache watching her struggle. My prayer for you and for me is this:

Lord, You know. You just do. All the aches and anxieties. All the worry and wondering. All the fears and feelings.

All of it. We need You and Your truth to shine bright in the haze and darkness. We long for You to give us clarity and wisdom. Give us insight into the hearts of our girls, and give us wisdom to guide them to You and the hope we have through You. It's easy for us to get lost in our feelings of insecurity and worry and fear and failure and doubt, but those don't come from You. As the hymnist wrote, "Tune my heart to sing Thy grace." When the world says "not enough," may we hear Your whispered assurance that You are enough. When the world points and proclaims "failure," draw us back to the truth that You have overcome, and that in You we also are more than conquerors. As we pray for our girls, as we intercede on their behalf and cry out for them to know the fullness of Your love and live it out for others to see You in them, may we also know these things for ourselves. Hold us close, Lord. We need You . . . and we long for You. In Jesus' name, Amen.[1]

Acknowledgments

The Lord be with your spirit. Grace be with you.

2 Timothy 4:22

Paul's words at the end of his second letter to Timothy are my favorite benediction. I have been fortunate to have a huge community of people who have encouraged, prayed for, and come alongside me. I'm immeasurably grateful to each of you.

Scott: You're my favorite! You believe in me when I can't believe in myself, and you've made every dream of my heart and every passion God has given me a possibility. Thank you for listening when I said we were supposed to get married. For over twenty years you've been making me laugh when I want to be mad and wiping the tears I try so hard to hide. No one will ever truly know the depth of sacrifice you have made for this project and for our incredible life—but I do. And there will never be enough days to say thank you. I love you. Always.

Casiday: You are my inspiration and joy! When we named you Hope, I had no idea the way God would use your life to restore the broken pieces of my own. I'm proud of who you are and inspired by the way you live. I look at you and wonder what I ever did to deserve the gift of being your mom. Wherever you go and whatever you do in this life, I pray you know this for certain: I am always and proudly Team Casiday.

Our families: What a gift to be born into a family that loves the Lord and has faithfully served Him for generations. To the Busters and Reagans who have loved me and nurtured my love of words since I was a little girl, thank you seems far too small, but it is all I know to say. To the Underwoods and Shirleys who welcomed me into their family over twenty years ago, thank you for loving me so well and believing in me.

Sandra, Stacey, and Brooke: This book really wouldn't be without the three of you. But far more important is this—my life is bigger and better because each of you is in it. As much as we love words, our hearts are bound by a deeper love for the Word-Made-Flesh. Of all the gifts the Internet has given me, our friendships are among the sweetest.

The "So You Wrote a Book" girls (Courtney D., Courtney W., Becky, Kristin, Karmen, Krista, and Megan): Y'all are the best kind of awesome! The little space where we share our deepest fears and our biggest dreams, where we wrestle through the balancing act of writing and living, is sacred and holy ground. I'm deeply thankful for it and for each of you.

My *Prayers for Girls* team (Amy, Beth, Brenda, Fayelle, and Lyndsey): What would I do without you? You've picked up the slack and prayed me through everything, and this book is better because of you. And to the whole Prayers for Girls community, girl moms are the best! The emails and texts and messages and prayers you generously gave throughout this whole process have been of immeasurable value, and I am humbled by your support.

Marguerite, Sheryl, Laura M., Laura B., Terri, and Paula: It goes without saying I have the best friends in the world! Thank you for believing in me, praying for me, and celebrating every little step.

Valerie, Paulee, and Meghan: Thank you for letting me share your stories. This book would be incomplete without them.

Ally, Ashleigh, Caitlan, Caroline, Haley, Madison, Morgan, and Tori: I love the boldness and enthusiasm you bring to my life. Every forty-five-year-old should have an incredible group of twentysomethings in her life! Thank you for asking me how the book was coming, for preordering copies, and for always making me smile. What would I do without our group texts and Bitmoji?

Janet Grant: When I think of you, the words of 1 Samuel 16:7 come to mind. Your willingness to value the heart of a writer over the appearance of a platform is a gift to all of us who are represented by you. I am grateful for your wisdom and guidance.

Jeff and the whole Bethany House team: Wow! Y'all are amazing. From cover design to copyediting and from manuscript to marketing, this whole experience has been flawless. Jeff, thank you for championing this project. Your encouragement and insight have made it far better than I could have imagined. I like to think if the Brauns and the Underwoods were neighbors our street would be the coolest in town.

And most of all, Jesus: For writing my story and allowing me the honor of sharing Yours. Eternity will not be long enough to give You praise and glory.

Notes

Chapter 1: The Girl in the Mirror

1. E. M. Bounds, *The Necessity of Prayer* (Palm Springs, CA: Merchant Books, 2015), 11.

2. Chris Nickson, "How a Young Generation Accepts Technology," November 29, 2016, http://www.atechnologysociety.co.uk/how-young-generation-accepts -technology.html.

3. "Definition—What Does *Digital Native* mean?" Technopedia, http://www .techopedia.com/definition/28094/digital-native.

Chapter 3: Loved

1. Emails exchanged with Meghan in October 2016.

Chapter 7: Kept

1. Definition from dictionary.com, http://www.dictionary.com/browse/keep ?s=t.

Chapter 8: Content

1. Pete Wilson, *Let Hope In: Four Choices that Will Change Your Life Forever* (Nashville: Thomas Nelson, 2013), 138.

2. Kristen Welch, *Raising Grateful Kids in an Entitled World* (Carol Stream, IL: Tyndale Momentum, 2015), 157.

Chapter 11: Renewed

1. Dictionary.com, http://www.dictionary.com/browse/percolate?s=t.

Chapter 12: Guarded

1. Anything but Ordinary, "Broken Hearts," http://bethbuster.blogspot.com /2014/05/broken-hearts.html

Chapter 16: Generosity

1. Read more about Kristen and her family's journey on her blog We Are THAT Family, www.wearethatfamily.com.

Chapter 19: Sanctification

1. Reprinted from my blog post, "A Prayer for My Girl as She Begins Her Sophomore Year." August 13, 2015, http://www.terilynneunderwood.com/2015/08 /a-prayer-for-my-girl-as-she-begins-her-sophomore-year/.

Chapter 23: P.S. A Note to the Mom Who Is Struggling

1. Prayer adapted from a Prayers for Girls email I sent January 25, 2016.

Teri Lynne Underwood leads Prayers for Girls, a popular online community for mothers, grandmothers, aunts, and anyone else who wants to invest in praying for the girls in their lives. A writer, ministry speaker, and Bible-study teacher, she is a frequent contributor to parenting blogs and is constantly on the hunt for ways to communicate truth with grace and, if possible, humor.

Teri Lynne is the daughter, granddaughter, and great-granddaughter (and now wife) of Southern Baptist pastors. Her husband, Scott, is the Minister of Music at Calvary Baptist Church in Russellville, Alabama. Their teenage daughter, Casiday, has given them equal parts great joy and gray hair. Life in a small town and in the fishbowl of ministry isn't always easy, but their little family of three can be regularly found making homemade pizza and watching episodes of their favorite television shows on Netflix. Learn more at www.terilynneunderwood.com.